Teaching for CHANGE in the ELA Classroom

This book can help you incorporate critical literacy pedagogy into your high school English Language Arts (ELA) classroom, so that your students can use what they study in class to work toward making a more just and equitable world.

Through the acronym CHANGE, the book explores how critical literacy pedagogy can support students as they Challenge injustice to Help make a difference in the world by Asking and answering tough questions and Noticing ways to Get involved and Engaged in making the world a better place. It first centers on the theory behind critical literacy pedagogy with Bob Fecho's concept of wobble, the tensions teachers experience when different points of view collide in the classroom, and why being mindful of and responding to moments of wobble can help educators grow in their teaching practice. The book then provides practical, specific suggestions by grade level for high school ELA teachers to implement critical literacy pedagogy in their classrooms, and address the tensions and moments of discomfort and uncertainty they might experience while providing critical literacy pedagogy.

With detailed lesson plans and case study examples from in-service ELA teachers, this book is an incredible resource for high school language arts teachers who are interested in teaching for social justice and integrating critical literacy pedagogy into their classrooms.

Dan Stockwell taught high school English language arts (ELA) in South Carolina for 8 years, and is now an assistant professor in the Department of English at California State University, Bakersfield, where he teaches courses for students studying to become secondary ELA teachers. His research focuses on how secondary ELA teachers can provide critical literacy pedagogy, even in restrictive contexts.

Also Available from Routledge Eye On Education
(www.routledge.com/eyeoneducation)

Teaching Reading and Literature with Classroom Talk: Dialogical Approaches and Practical Strategies in the Secondary ELA Classroom
Dawan Coombs

Teach This Poem, Volume I: The Natural World
Madeleine Fuchs Holzer and The Academy of American Poets

Student-Centered Literacy Assessment in the 6-12 Classroom: An Asset-Based Approach
Sean Ruday

Grammar Inquiries, Grades 6–12: An Inquiry- and Asset-Based Approach to Grammar Instruction
Sean Ruday

The Antiracist English Language Arts Classroom
Keisha Rembert

The Literacy Coaching Handbook: Working With Teachers to Increase Student Achievement, 2nd edition
Diana Sisson and Betsy Sisson

Teaching for CHANGE in the ELA Classroom: Integrating Social Justice and Critical Literacy for Grades 9–12
Dan Stockwell

Teaching for CHANGE in the ELA Classroom
Integrating Social Justice and Critical Literacy for Grades 9–12

Dan Stockwell

Routledge
Taylor & Francis Group
NEW YORK AND LONDON

Designed cover image: © Getty Images

First published 2025
by Routledge
605 Third Avenue, New York, NY 10158

and by Routledge
4 Park Square, Milton Park, Abingdon, Oxon, OX14 4RN

Routledge is an imprint of the Taylor & Francis Group, an informa business

© 2025 Dan Stockwell

The right of Dan Stockwell to be identified as author of this work has been asserted in accordance with sections 77 and 78 of the Copyright, Designs and Patents Act 1988.

All rights reserved. No part of this book may be reprinted or reproduced or utilised in any form or by any electronic, mechanical, or other means, now known or hereafter invented, including photocopying and recording, or in any information storage or retrieval system, without permission in writing from the publishers.

Trademark notice: Product or corporate names may be trademarks or registered trademarks, and are used only for identification and explanation without intent to infringe.

ISBN: 978-1-032-81442-1 (hbk)
ISBN: 978-1-032-81441-4 (pbk)
ISBN: 978-1-003-50017-9 (ebk)

DOI: 10.4324/9781003500179

Typeset in Palatino
by SPi Technologies India Pvt Ltd (Straive)

To Samantha Stockwell who forever changed my life.

Contents

Meet the Author ix
Acknowledgements xi

Introduction 1

1 What is Critical Literacy Pedagogy in ELA? 6

2 What is Wobble? 24

3 What is *Stretchiness*? 47

4 What Could Critical Literacy Pedagogy Look Like in Grade 9? 67

5 What Could Critical Literacy Pedagogy Look Like in Grade 10? 96

6 What Could Critical Literacy Pedagogy Look Like in Grade 11? 126

7 What Could Critical Literacy Pedagogy Look Like in Grade 12? 160

8 Conclusion 187

*Appendix A: Suggestions for Teaching for CHANGE
in English Language Arts* 194

*Appendix B: Example Letter to Parents and Guardians
about Your Plans for the R&J Issues Unit* 198

*Appendix C: Example Letter to Parents or Guardians
about Your Plans for the Speaking into the Silence Unit*......202

*Appendix D: Example Letter to Parents or Guardians
about Your Plans for the Environmental Justice Unit*........206

*Appendix E: Example Letter to Parents or Guardians
about Your Plans for the Postcolonial Literature Unit*........209

Meet the Author

Dan Stockwell has been an educator for over a decade, first as a high school English language arts (ELA) teacher in South Carolina for eight years and now as an assistant professor of English Education at California State University, Bakersfield (CSUB). Dan is passionate about public education and advocates for teachers and students. Because of the recent increased encroachment on teacher professionalism and autonomy and because of increased efforts to ban books and censor classroom discourse, through his teaching and research, Dan aims to advance the goals of critical literacy pedagogy and to support teachers in engaging their students in critical literacy themselves so they can change the world to make it more equitable and just.

Dan decided to resign from teaching high school to pursue his PhD after the 2018–2019 academic year. Even back then, he was required to teach a set curriculum, and his autonomy regarding text selection was limited: Because of recent laws passed in South Carolina, though, Dan knows that lessons he used to teach that addressed issues of race and racism could now be considered illegal. Dan's research specifically focuses on how teachers can implement critical literacy pedagogy, even if they teach in restrictive contexts.

Dan also knows that his past advocacy for his students could be considered illegal. When he taught high school ELA, Dan was asked to sponsor his school's Genders and Sexualities Alliance Club (GSA; formerly known as the Gay-Straight Alliance) by a former student. Dan was thrilled to co-sponsor his school's GSA club along with the school librarian until he resigned to pursue his PhD. He is devastated to know that bills being considered in South Carolina could make it illegal for teachers to sponsor such clubs. Much of *Teaching for CHANGE in the ELA Classroom* was inspired by Dan's recognition that lessons he used to teach and activism he was happy to engage in might now be considered illegal by misguided legislators.

As second author, Dan has cowritten a book chapter, "Student Voice Is Power: Incorporating Critical Witness and Testimony in Middle-School Classrooms," published in Routledge's *Connecting Theory and Practice in Middle School Literacy: Critical Conversations*. As third author, Dan has cowritten an article, "The Impact of Analyzing Young Adult Literature for Racial Identity / Social Justice Orientation with Interdisciplinary Students," published by the *Journal of College Reading and Learning*. Recently, Dan wrote the article, "Retaking the Teaching Profession: A Case for Being Brave," published in the *English Journal*.

Dan is a member of the National Council of Teachers of English (NCTE) and the California Association of Teachers of English. In November 2024, Dan began his term serving on the NCTE's secondary section steering committee. At CSUB, Dan serves his department as one of the co-sponsors of English Club. His main contribution to the English Club has been to run sessions of the role-playing game *Dungeons & Dragons* for English majors seeking to escape, if only for a few hours, the realities of being a college student.

In his free time, Dan loves to spend time with his spouse Samantha and their dog Sybil. Together, they enjoy long walks in the park. Samantha and Dan also enjoy playing board games inspired by novels and playing *Dungeons & Dragons* together.

Introduction

This is a book for secondary English language arts (ELA) teachers who are interested in providing instruction that supports social justice efforts and engages youth in critical literacy. If you are teaching now or are studying to become a teacher, you may have noticed that much of the current discourse surrounding teaching can be quite negative and discouraging. In recent years, teachers have seen their profession maligned for various reasons (e.g., how public education systems responded to the COVID-19 pandemic and how specific schools underperformed on standardized tests), but the criticism that troubles me most is that some detractors accuse teachers of indoctrination or of harming youth when their teaching addresses issues and topics such as the history of the United States, race and racism, genders and sexualities, rights for members of LGBTQIA+ communities, and social justice. More and more, legislators are passing laws meant to silence those with whom they disagree ideologically and to control classroom discourse.

This is troubling to me because I am an educator. Now, I am an assistant professor of English Education, and my undergraduate students are studying to become secondary ELA teachers soon. I want them to graduate and work in positive, encouraging environments. I want my students to be respected as the professionals they are becoming. I don't want them to graduate after spending years preparing creative lessons that will excite and engage youth only to teach in restrictive contexts that prescribe their curricula and disrespect them and the entire teaching profession. Before I became an assistant professor, I taught high school ELA for eight years. I loved teaching secondary ELA, but when I had opportunities to serve as a cooperative teacher for college students as they completed their teaching internships, I discovered a passion for supporting ELA teachers. So I resigned from teaching to pursue my PhD in 2019. When I was teaching high school, some of this negative discourse surrounding public school teaching existed, of course, but the attacks on the teaching profession increased during the pandemic and as politically conservative legislators and activists decided that classroom teachers and school librarians needed to be the targets of their vitriol. In my PhD program, I studied Critical Race Theory, critical theory, and critical literacy. Just as I was learning exciting concepts and theory that could influence my teaching practice and that I believed could make schooling more relevant, meaningful, and equitable for all youth, I witnessed the rise in attacks on teachers and the teaching profession. I watched in disgust and desperation as the state legislators where I used to teach, South Carolina, considered bills that would make lessons I taught in the past illegal today because they upheld the view that racism occurs daily in U.S. society. Just as I saw the need for and the incredible potential of critical literacy pedagogy (CLP) that advocated for social justice, equity, and change, there was a surge in politically conservative states to outlaw the "teaching of Critical Race Theory" and to reduce teachers' autonomy regarding which texts and topics they are allowed to explore with students in their classrooms.

This book is my response to these attacks on public school teachers and their profession, and in it I offer encouragement to support secondary ELA teachers in their attempts to promote social justice and teach for CHANGE. CHANGE is an acronym I created to explain the heart of social justice and CLP: teaching for CHANGE is about supporting students as they Challenge injustice to Help make a difference in the world by Asking and answering tough questions and Noticing ways to Get involved and Engaged in making the world a better place.

This book is divided into two parts. Part 1 is based on my high school teaching experience, the published literature and research on CLP in secondary ELA classrooms, critical theory, and the qualitative study I conducted for my dissertation. I used qualitative methods like classroom observations, audio-recorded interviews, artifact collection, and debriefing conversations to conduct case studies of secondary ELA teachers to understand their experiences with tension, doubt, and fear as they attempted to provide CLP in sociopolitically restrictive contexts. Part 1 poses and answers important questions to define key terms, explains (in general) how secondary ELA teachers can teach for CHANGE, and describes the findings and insights from my research with practicing secondary ELA teachers.

Chapter 1 defines terms like *critical literacy* and *critical literacy pedagogy* and explores more deeply what it means to teach for CHANGE with secondary ELA curricula. The first chapter also explains, briefly, the theory behind CLP and offers suggestions for implementing CLP in secondary ELA. The second chapter describes the study I conducted with practicing ELA teachers as I investigated their experiences as they provided CLP. Using the teachers' own words and reflections, Chapter 2 focuses on the tension, doubt, and fears that the participants experienced and that other secondary ELA teachers likely experience too. Chapter 3, the last chapter of Part 1, returns to the teachers from my study to examine lessons learned from their experiences and responses to the fear and doubt they navigated. The third chapter also encourages teachers to remain committed to providing CLP despite the tensions they experience as they teach for CHANGE.

Part 2 of this book is also based on theory, findings and insights from my dissertation research, and my teaching experience, but Part 2 offers practical and actionable advice and suggestions for secondary ELA teachers interested in teaching for CHANGE.Chapters 4, 5, 6, and 7 explore in detail the potentials for CLP in grades 9 to 12, with one chapter dedicated to each grade. Each chapter begins with an overview of what teachers are already doing in these grades to teach for CHANGE. Next, these chapters discuss other possibilities for teaching for CHANGE based on the curricula traditionally taught in each of these grades. Then, for each grade, I describe an instructional unit I created to support you in providing CLP that encourages social justice. These chapters include 10 lesson plans for each unit that you can apply to your current teaching. Finally, these chapters conclude with advice and encouragement based on findings from my dissertation research to help you navigate the tensions you may experience as you teach for CHANGE with the suggested units.

Chapter 4 addresses traditional 9th-grade curricula, and the suggested unit focuses on Shakespeare's *Romeo and Juliet*. In this unit, students will read Shakespeare and a challenged young adult novel of their choice to decide for themselves what is appropriate or not for them to study in school. This unit challenges the current push to ban and censor books. Chapter 5 focuses on grade 10 ELA curricula, which usually involve the study of different texts connected by a common theme like coming of age or identity. The unit for this chapter focuses on Ibi Zoboi's young adult novel *American Street* and supports students in researching curricular and historical silences so they can resist the ways that people, their cultures, and their histories are being silenced by states passing laws controlling classroom discourse on issues like racism. Because grade 11 ELA curricula traditionally emphasize the study of America literature, Chapter 6 presents a unit on Helena María Viramontes's novel *Under the Feet of Jesus*, which like John Steinbeck's *Of Mice and Men*, takes place in California and focuses on farm workers in the fields. The unit engages students in investigating injustices, present in the novel, that still occur today, and it supports them in researching what they can do to address these injustices. Chapter 7 presents a different approach to teaching British literature, which is often taught to seniors: The suggested unit teaches postcolonial literary theory and focuses on Zimbabwean author Tsitsi Dangarembga's novel *The Book of Not*. As students read this novel and apply postcolonial theory to their study of the book, they will inquire into what brings humans happiness and fulfillment, and the goal of this unit is for seniors to consider what changes they need to help make in the world so that it is more just and equitable. Of course, your ELA curriculum might differ from what I've described for each of these grades, but please consider how you could adjust the units as needed to fit your teaching context.

The final chapter offers additional encouragement for secondary ELA teachers to continue teaching for CHANGE. I hope you'll find the theory and insights from my study that are discussed in Part 1 instructive. I hope you'll find the units and lesson plans described in Part 2 useful in your teaching. I also hope this book encourages you because teaching for CHANGE is extremely difficult, but it is crucial to making the world more just. Most importantly, I hope this book inspires you as you and your students change the world!

1

What is Critical Literacy Pedagogy in ELA?

If you've looked through the Table of Contents, you've probably noticed that the title of every chapter, except for the final one, is a question. Of course, that's on purpose. Any personal growth I've made as a human and educator has occurred through questioning and reflection. Often, it was my students' questions that helped me identify ways I could grow and improve in my teaching practice.

I remember one question, in particular. I used to teach Arthur Miller's *The Crucible*. One day, we were reading Act I, and Adam, who was a joy to teach, was chatting with a classmate. I walked over to his desk and asked him to pay attention as his classmates read their assigned roles for the day. Adam, meaning no disrespect, looked at me and asked, "But what are we learning?" I had to stop myself from answering, "We're learning the plot of the play." Truly, that's what we were doing, for I had not really designed an exciting lesson that engaged students in doing anything beyond remembering what John Proctor and Abigail Williams did in the barn. We were simply reading the play and taking notes that day. There is nothing wrong with reading a play and taking notes, but I could have made the lesson more meaningful to my students. The kind of pedagogy I'm advocating for in this book, critical literacy pedagogy (CLP), aims to engage students in meaningful learning. It is my hope that once you've read this book and applied it to your teaching, your students won't have to wonder, like Adam did in my class, if what they're doing is meaningful to them.

Looking back, I believe Adam's question implied he didn't see the value in or need to spend several class periods listening to his friends struggle through Miller's imitation of 17th-century Puritan English. He could simply read a summary, watch any number of videos online explaining the plot of *The Crucible*, or pay attention when I showed the film in class. Adam wanted to know the point—what was the point of reading this play, which was produced in the 20th century, about historical events from the 17th century with commentary on the Red Scare in the 20th, when he's living in the 21st century? When I realized I could not come up with a compelling answer to his question on the spot, I knew I needed to reflect and grow in my teaching practice. Now that I'm an assistant professor who focuses on preparing future secondary English language arts (ELA) teachers, I continue to think about Adam's question.

Reflective questions I've asked myself have helped me grow, too. Am I meeting my students' needs? All of my students' needs or just the ones who already really like to read and discuss theme and character development? What do I believe is the ultimate purpose of ELA instruction—to make sure students can accomplish all the standards? To prepare students for a standardized test? To help students graduate and enter the workforce, where they are told their worth comes from how much money they make and many employers don't care if they can analyze how a poet used figurative language or irony to convey a theme? To help students enjoy literature, even if they're going to graduate into a world that will demand they work so hard they probably won't have time much to sit down with a good book? To force students to read books that don't reflect them or their experiences? Or is there a deeper purpose for ELA teachers and the things we do every day with students in our classrooms?

These are some tough questions. As educators, asking ourselves questions is a way we can grow in our teaching practice, even if we don't immediately have all the answers. That's why the chapters in this book are questions. I hope the questions this book poses will help you reflect on your teaching practice and will help you grow as well. So, on to the first question.

What is Critical Literacy Pedagogy?

This first question requires a shared understanding of three key terms: *critical*, *literacy*, and *pedagogy*. These terms have lots of definitions, so I will start by providing clear definitions for how these terms will be used in this book.

First, people often use the word *critical* when talking about critical thinking. Critical thinking, according to Glaser (1941), requires three things: (1) a desire to thoughtfully approach problems, (2) knowledge of how to inquire and reason, and (3) "some skill in applying" that knowledge (p. 6). Glaser argued that public schooling needed to prepare students to become "an enlightened and competent citizenry" (p. 4) by helping them develop and practice critical thinking. I view Glaser's understanding of critical thinking as evaluative thinking. When *critical* is used in this way, it means the kind of thinking that judges something, like an author's argument, and asks if it measures up to a criterion. While there may be slight overlap, I'm not using the word *critical* the same way Glaser does.

I'm using the word to denote a particular way of reading texts, thinking about them, producing them, and using them to act in the world. In this way, of course, to read critically involves evaluating. It involves thoughtfully approaching problems that affect our students' lives. It demands a questioning disposition that constantly seeks to understand how power is used and abused. When I use the word *critical*, I'm referring to the critical tradition of philosophy as expressed in critical theory.

Ernest Morrell has written an excellent book titled *Critical Literacy and Urban Youth: Pedagogies of Access, Dissent, and Liberation*. Morrell (2008) summarizes thousands of years of philosophy to help educators understand the theoretical foundations of critical literacy and how that can impact their secondary ELA instruction today. My research with secondary ELA teachers is inspired by Morrell's book, and below I'll summarize what

I've learned from him to explain how I use the term *critical* in this book.

Morrell began his review of the philosophical foundations of critical theory with the classic Greek philosophers. He describes how after the Roman empire collapsed and the European "Dark Ages" began, European philosophers, educators, and artists eventually rediscovered ancient philosophy and art. The Renaissance came about as a "re-engagement" with the works of the ancient philosophers (and artisans) and ultimately lead to the age of the Enlightenment in Western philosophy (Morrell, 2008, p. 36).

The Enlightenment was a time of questioning. As philosophers, scientists, artists, teachers, and thinkers interacted with classical works, they rebelled against the Catholic Church, which at the time had a monopoly on religious and cultural thought in Europe. The Enlightenment thinkers challenged Church doctrine and practices, and they questioned the nature of knowledge and who gets to decide what counts as knowledge.

These thinkers influenced Karl Marx. You don't have to be a Marxist (or any kind of "ist") to teach for CHANGE. Though I am not an economist, journalist, or revolutionary (Marx was all of these), I am an educator, and I'm deeply passionate about helping students use texts in meaningful ways so they don't have to ask me, like Adam did, "What are we learning?" I want what I do in the classroom with students to matter to them, and I think CLP is a great way to make what we do in classrooms meaningful to youth. The work of Karl Marx is important for educators who want to help students find what we do in ELA classrooms useful and meaningful.

As Morrell explained, Marx was influenced by the Enlightenment thinkers, and he encouraged readers to adopt a certain "attitude toward texts" and a certain way of reading texts (p. 41). He wanted readers to be aware that texts often convey ideologies, and usually the ideologies that belong to those with (and in) power are the dominant ideologies, the ones being printed and consumed by people with less power and influence. Marx wanted people with less influence and power to read critically, not just evaluatively, but critically—he wanted them to be aware that the texts they consumed did not represent neutral, disinterested, unchallengeable knowledge but ideology-laden "knowledge" designed, at least at times, to oppress them. Marx encouraged readers to question and challenge texts instead of believing everything they read—just like the Renaissance artists challenged the Catholic Church. Readers familiar with the book *Pedagogy of the Oppressed* (1970/2018) by Brazilian philosopher and educator Paulo Freire can probably recognize the influence of Marx. Marx helped bring critical thought into the 19th century. People who came after him, like Freire, brought it into the 20th century.

According to Freire (1970/2018), by reading texts critically and engaging in civic and political action, people can come to understand the social, political, and economic workings of the world around them and can strive together to transform the world to be more equitable and just. Coming to this understanding is called developing "sociopolitical consciousness" (Dyches, 2018b, p. 38). Freire and his colleague Donaldo Macedo described the kind of reading that leads to sociopolitical consciousness as reading the word and the world (Freire & Macedo, 1987). Reading the word and the world means using texts to learn about the world and then using texts to work toward making the world better.

Reading the word and the world involves "praxis," which Freire (1970/2018) defined as "reflection and action upon the world in order to transform it" (p. 51). While praxis is not easy to do, and it is certainly not easy to implement in ELA classrooms, my stance is that the ultimate purpose of ELA is to support students in praxis, so they can use what they study in ELA classrooms to take action to make their communities (and ultimately the world) more equitable and more just. I believe ELA instruction should support students in reading and (re)writing the world. This belief is the heart of teaching for CHANGE.

Many theorists, researchers, and educators have further developed critical theory in the 21st century (see hooks, 1994; Janks, 2012). As a quick note, critical scholar and professor bell hooks was greatly influenced by Freire, but hooks challenged Freire's sexist language as she worked to advance feminist thought in the 20th and 21st centuries. Obviously, it is not difficult to see how the ideas of Karl Marx, who encouraged people to challenge dominant ideologies, align with the ideas of feminist theorists, like hooks, who reject sexism and the sexist messages women often receive. For now, though, I think I've provided enough of an overview to define *critical*. I've included additional resources at the end of this chapter for readers interested in learning more about critical theory as it relates to educating and inspiring youth.

In this book, *critical* refers to reading, writing, thinking, speaking, and doing inspired by the critical theory I've briefly discussed. Critical anything (reading, writing, thinking, speaking, listening, producing, and doing) is about asking questions of the messages and perspectives in the texts we consume, who benefits from those messages or perspectives, and what other messages or perspectives could counter the dominant ones. Critical anything is a way of approaching ideas and ideologies in the texts we read and the media we consume. Though Glaser's (1941) understanding of critical thinking was not based on critical philosophy, our understandings agree on this point: The important thing is a person's attitude and disposition. Critical thinking and critical literacy, as they will be used and discussed in this book, require educators and our students to have certain attitudes and dispositions toward the word and the world.

The critical way of approaching texts encourages us to challenge messages we receive, and it reminds us that we don't have to be passive consumers and absorbers. We should be active so we can call out problems and injustices and work toward making the world a better place (i.e., reading and writing the world). The critical approach to texts reminds us that we can be more than objects of someone else's designs. We can be subjects. We can make a difference. We can be agents of change.

Now, on to how I'll use the word *literacy* in this book. Obviously, the word has something to do with reading and writing, but the way it is often used can obscure its meaning. The way I use the word literacy in this book is quite simple: Literacy is what "people do with literacy" (Barton & Hamilton, 2000, p. 7). That may be deceptively simple, so I'll provide an example. I've heard people talk about having (or not having) financial literacy. I imagine that financial literacy probably means something along the lines of "knowing how to save, invest, and increase wealth."

Financial literacy involves reading specific texts (texts probably only experts in the field or people with a lot to gain/lose could want to read), and it involves not only understanding how to read and write those kinds of texts, not only how to accomplish the goal of increasing wealth, but also doing certain behaviors needed to secure and increase it. Back to Barton and Hamilton's definition of *literacy*: It is "what people do with literacy" (p. 7). We can see the truth to that simple definition: Financial literacy is what a person does to accomplish their goals, so a person with financial literacy performs their financial literacy. They do it. They read and write and think and behave and do—they perform their literacy.

Because lots of different people for different, specific reasons are performing their literacies, literacy scholars recognize the word has come to mean demonstrating proficiency, skill, and an insider's know-how with specific texts, technologies, or ways of thinking and behaving in order to accomplish specific goals (see Gee, 2015; Scribner & Cole, 1981; Street, 1984). I am indebted to Sylvia Scribner and Michael Cole and their book *The Psychology of Literacy* for this understanding of *literacy*. I am also indebted to the authors I cited above who are proponents of sociocultural perspectives of language, literacy, and learning for helping me see that literacy is a "cover-term" (Gee, 2015, p. 45) for the things people do with and surrounding texts. In this book, *literacy* means the things people do with texts and technologies, including the ways people think as they use texts, technologies, and knowledge to accomplish their goals, so it is plural (see Street, 1994). If people are doing something with texts to accomplish specific goals, they are engaging in literacies. Literacies are verbs.

To answer the first question of this book—What is CLP?—I still need to define pedagogy. This last term should be the easiest one to define. Like literacy, *pedagogy* is a broad term, and it too involves actions—verbs. It refers to the things teachers do in the classroom as they teach. Simply, *pedagogy* is what a teacher does to teach their subject.

While the word *pedagogy* is simple to define, the concept is quite complex and, as I'm sure you know, quite difficult to perform. My views of pedagogy are highly influenced by researcher and professor Django Paris. Paris's concept of culturally sustaining pedagogy (CSP) advocates for critical and democratic approaches to teaching, and as Paris (2012) defined it, CSP seeks "to perpetuate and foster—to sustain—linguistic, literate, and cultural pluralism as part of the democratic project of schooling" (p. 95; see also Paris & Alim, 2014, 2017). Paris's concept of CSP reminds educators that, while *pedagogy* means the things teachers do to teach, it includes ways of thinking about and approaching teaching and students. What people do is influenced by their values, by the thinking they've been enculturated into, by their experiences, and by a host of other factors. Pedagogy includes teachers' attitudes toward the subject they teach, the students they teach, what they think is most important for their students to know and do, what they were trained to do in their teacher-preparation programs, how teachers decide to plan and implement lessons, their views of texts (especially, which texts are worth studying in school and which ones are not), and their views of learning and, therefore, teaching.

Now, let's bring these three terms together to define *critical literacy pedagogy*. CLP is what teachers do to engage their students in thinking, reading, writing, speaking, discussing, and producing in critical ways so their students can engage in literacy geared toward reading and rewriting the word and the world (i.e., using literacy to learn about the world and act in it to make it better). When students use literacies to challenge, critique, question, and wonder how they can act to make the world more just, they are engaging in critical literacy. When a teacher designs a lesson to engage students in critical literacy, they are providing CLP. Because I'm advocating that high school ELA teachers use their CLP to engage their students in critical literacy, I want to define CLP using language meant to inspire youth: CLP is what teachers do in the classroom (and maybe outside of it as well) to encourage students to speak to, speak back to, and speak against abuses of power and issues of injustice.

Speaking to Power and Injustice

When teachers support students in recognizing the role that power plays in society and in the texts that societies produce and consume, they are helping students speak to power. For example, teachers can provide CLP to help students see that the texts most often studied in American literature classes are written mostly by White men. This supports students in speaking to this power. It helps them realize that racism, sexism, and classism have resulted in narrow curricula because certain people had the power (and privilege) to write and publish, and it helps them realize that curricula could be different. The way curricula are is not the only way they can be designed. As professor and researcher Hilary Janks (2005) has argued, all texts are *positioned* and *positioning*. They are positioned because authors are in a place of power, and they are positioning because they put readers in a position designed to convince them of the writer's points of view. Supporting students in speaking to power and injustice engages them in reading the world surrounding them. That's a great start, but the CLP I'm advocating for in this book wants to do more than simply raise awareness about issues related to power.

Speaking Back to and Against Power and Injustice

Once youth speak to power, ELA teachers can support them in speaking back to it and against the injustices that stem from abuses of power. For example, professor and researcher Jeanne Dyches worked with a high school ELA teacher to engage their students in speaking back to power and injustice. They implemented an injustice mini-unit with the purpose of challenging the curriculum that emphasized some large-scale injustices while ignoring others. During the mini-unit, students supplemented their curriculum by researching some of the mass injustices it ignored, and Dyches stated this helped them "feel more agentive and empowered to push back against" curricular constraints (2018a, p. 245). In Dyches's study, the students spoke back to power when they not only became aware of the issue of power at hand (i.e., people create curricula, and they have the power to influence what is studied and what is not studied in school) but also realized they could do something about it. They spoke back against their narrow curriculum when they self-selected and researched other injustices they felt should have been included all along in their world literature class. They spoke back against power and injustice when they realized they could make a meaningful CHANGE to their curriculum.

Teaching for CHANGE in the English Classroom

I've created the acronym CHANGE to help educators think about how they can implement CLP in their classrooms. CLP supports students as they Challenge injustice to Help make a difference in the world by Asking and answering tough questions and Noticing ways to Get involved and Engaged in making the world a better place. CLP is what teachers do to encourage their students to work to CHANGE the world. CLP is what teachers do to teach for CHANGE. I'll use these words interchangeably in the rest of this book: Teaching for CHANGE is providing CLP, and if you're providing CLP, you're teaching for CHANGE. Teaching for CHANGE requires constant self-reflection and evaluation. (See Appendix A for suggestions to guide you in these processes.)

If you're thinking that teaching for CHANGE sounds extremely challenging, I completely agree. CLP is difficult (or even scary) to implement, especially in states where even talking about racism with students in class might be illegal (see Sykes & Hinger, 2021). The point of this book is not to act like CLP is easy or to make you feel that what you're currently doing in the classroom is not enough and that you must provide CLP (as I've defined it and as I'll advocate for in later chapters of this book) right now or else you're a terrible teacher and person. That's not the point.

The point of this book is to encourage you to teach for CHANGE. I hope to do that by raising important questions; providing some answers and insight based on research, personal experiences, and teacher reflections; and offering specific lesson plan suggestions you can use in your teaching. I don't have all (or even most) of the answers, but I have a desire to make ELA instruction more valuable for students. I have a desire to encourage students to make the world a better place, one text and one assignment at a time. I have a desire for students to see themselves as social agents with power to make a difference in the world, as they speak to, speak back to, and speak against abuses of power and injustice. This book aims to encourage you as you work to support your students in advocating for needed CHANGE. I believe ELA teachers have a lot to offer students and therefore the world. I'm inspired and excited by the potential of ELA! Even though providing CLP is challenging, I think it is worth doing, and I'm excited to explore ways of making it happen in ELA classrooms. So, on to the next question.

How Can Critical Literacy Pedagogy be Implemented in ELA?

The definition of literacy I use in this book recognizes literacy as certain actions or practices (Gee, 2015). As you know, there are things "English people" do with texts that are unique to the subject of ELA. Reading and interpreting a sonnet require different literacies than reading and interpreting scientific data in a report or textbook. The actions a person does when they use texts to accomplish their goals are specific to each subject. Because literacy is specific to each subject (see Moje, 2015; Rainey, 2017), ELA teachers will enact CLP in ELA-specific ways. Here is a list of things that secondary ELA teachers can do to implement CLP in their classrooms. (It is inspired by Morrell's book *Critical Literacy and Urban Youth: Pedagogies of Access, Dissent, and Liberation*.)

- Help students recognize that texts like short stories and novels can promote dominant ideologies that discriminate against and marginalize people who were traditionally prevented from publishing their works
- Encourage students to speak back to power by challenging the traditional canon of their grade's curriculum
- Guide students in challenging the harmful ideologies they encounter in the texts studied in school
- Inspire students to ask difficult questions about the way the world works in the texts they study and how needed change can be effected through students' writing and action
- Use texts studied in class as tools to challenge abuses of power and injustices
- Teach students literary theories, like feminism and postcolonialism, and help them use those theories to interpret texts from critical perspectives

- Give students meaningful opportunities to learn and practice the art of rhetoric so they can advocate for a more just world
- Support students in using literacy practices like writing and rhetoric to take action to make their worlds more equitable, or help students use creative writing to rewrite pieces of literature studied in school to be more equitable and just
- Encourage students to use the literacies they engage in daily as valued ways of making and communicating knowledge in the classroom (e.g., students can demonstrate their awareness of audience and purpose by creating and posting TikTok videos).

This challenging but inspiring list can be summed up thusly: CLP in ELA occurs when teachers provide instruction that helps students read and (re)write the word and the world. To rewrite the world means using the kinds of writing and performance valued in ELA to advocate for a better, more just world. If your teaching does that, you're providing CLP.

You can accomplish the items on the list (and much, much more) in your teaching. As you select novels to study to you help students determine their themes, you can select texts whose themes speak to and against the abuse of power and injustices that are relevant to your students. As you prepare your syllabi, you can intentionally include works by diverse authors so your curricula don't communicate harmful messages about whose works are worthy (and whose are not) of study. When you prepare to teach argumentative writing, you can think of ways to help students write (and share) their arguments on important topics that matter to them. Your teaching can help students learn the skills and literacies valued in ELA as well as learn how to use those skills and literacies for CHANGE.

This seems like a great place for an important note: I am a reflective educator, so I always think back on my teaching and consider ways I could improve. Reflecting on how I used to teach high school ELA, I've identified many times when my teaching missed opportunities to engage students in critical literacy. I can't help but feel I should have done more, and I wish I could go back, knowing what I've learned since then about critical theory, to improve my teaching and to engage my students in critical literacy. I want to go back and teach for CHANGE. Part of being a reflective educator means I can, at times, forget to practice compassion toward my past self. So, if you're feeling down on yourself or are overwhelmed because of anything I've written so far, I'm sorry. I don't want to make anyone feel judged or discouraged. Instead, I want readers to be encouraged to engage in this difficult but essential work. Providing CLP is not easy, and there is no single correct way to do it. It's not about being perfect, it's about working with our students, one lesson at a time, to make the world a better place.

Why is Critical Literacy Pedagogy Important?

CLP is important because if secondary ELA teachers are not intentional with what they do in the classroom, injustices can be reproduced. Adolescents live in an unjust world, where they are often oppressed and marginalized by those in power. The texts produced and valued by those in power are ideology-laden, and they often convey harmful messages to students. If these texts are studied uncritically in classrooms, students might even accept and repeat these harmful messages. CLP is important so that injustices students read about are not perpetuated in secondary ELA classrooms.

I don't think any teacher wants injustices to be reproduced in their classroom, and being critically intentional with lesson planning and pedagogy reduces this possibility. I am inspired by scholar and professor Yolanda Sealey-Ruiz, who encourages educators to "engage in a self-work and reflection on their practice that allows them to interrupt the status quo of inequity in our schools" (2022, p. 21). Sealey-Ruiz warns that "if teachers do not critically examine themselves and their practice, they are likely to continue enacting a pedagogy that harms instead of heals"

(p. 25). I never intended to harm any of my students, but when I reflect on my teaching, I can point out times my pedagogy did not heal either. A CLP approach to teaching encourages us to question, challenge, and be alert to possible harmful messages and to engage students in pushing back against these injustices. It encourages us to support students in speaking to, speaking back to, and speaking against these injustices that fill the pages of the texts studied in schools. Adopting a CLP helps educators teach for CHANGE and for healing as well.

CLP is also important because it can make what students study in ELA classrooms meaningful to them. I think back to my student Adam (mentioned at the beginning of this chapter), who asked, "But what are we learning?" when we were reading *The Crucible*. My instruction was not meaningful for him. If I had implemented CLP while we studied the play, though, I doubt Adam would have asked that question.

Here is what I would do now if I were still teaching this play: Because Miller wrote it, in part, to criticize some pretty serious injustices occurring during the Red Scare, I would engage students in doing something similar. I would ask them to brainstorm some injustices or issues in society that were important to them. Then I would require them to investigate that injustice that mattered most to them. Once their research was complete, I would have students imitate the way Miller infused his creative writing with social critique. Students would be tasked with using their research to produce creative or expository writing to advocate for needed change. Adam, who played football, may have wanted to investigate injustices related to athletics, and if I had used the play as an example of what writers can do to speak out against injustice and supported students in doing something similar with their own writing, I bet Adam would have felt he was actually learning something meaningful in my class. Making learning meaningful and important to students in ELA classrooms, something CLP does, is good teaching because "real reading and real writing for real audiences and real purposes" are among the best practices for ELA instruction (Bruce, 2013, p. 32). Providing CLP in ELA classrooms is important because it is good teaching.

The most important reason I could ever come up with, though, is that CLP is what is right for our students, all students, but especially our students who are often racialized and otherwise marginalized in schools and society. In the United States, students of color make up the majority of students in public schools (Paris & Alim, 2017). Not in every classroom but in many classrooms across the U.S., students of color are viewed from deficit perspectives, and they and their literacies are devalued (see Baker-Bell, 2020; Kirkland, 2013; Paris & Alim, 2017). A CLP approach to teaching ELA encourages teachers to push back against oppressive forces that devalue students and instead supports students in using their literacies to advocate for a better world.

CLP is all about supporting students as they become "powerful readers and writers of the word and the world" (Morrell, 2017, p. 459). I believe CLP is important, specifically for ELA teachers, because teachers can support their students in reading the world and rewriting it. Teaching for CHANGE engages students in advocating for and working toward social justice. Ernest Morrell argued "there is no higher social calling, no work more honorable" for ELA teachers than providing CLP (2005, p. 312). I wholeheartedly agree, and in this book, I hope to encourage you to engage in this honorable work as you teach for CHANGE.

Recommended Resources on Critical Theory and Literacy

- Alim, H. S. (2007). Critical hip-hop language pedagogies: Combat, consciousness, and the cultural politics of communication. *Journal of Language, Identity & Education, 6*(2), 161–176. https://doi.org/10.1080/15348450701341378
- Fairclough, N. (2015). *Language and power* (3rd ed.). Routledge.
- Johnson, L. J. (2022). *Critical race English education: New visions, new possibilities*. Routledge.
- Ladson-Billings, G. (1995). Toward a theory of culturally relevant pedagogy. *American Educational Research Journal, 32*(3), 465–491.

- Luke, A. (2012). Critical literacy: Foundational notes. *Theory into Practice, 51*(4), 4–11. https://doi.org/10.1080/00405841.2012.636324
- Shor, I. (1992). *Empowering education: Critical teaching for social change.* University of Chicago Press.
- Vasquez, V. M., Janks, H., & Comber, B. (2019). Critical literacy as a way of being and doing. *Language Arts, 95*(5), 300–311.

References

Baker-Bell, A. (2020). *Linguist justice: Black Language, literacy, identity, and pedagogy.* Routledge.

Barton, D. & Hamilton, M. (2000). Literacy practices. In D. Barton, M. Hamilton, & R. Ivanič (Eds.), *Situated literacies: Reading and writing in context* (pp. 7–16). Routledge.

Bruce, H. E. (2013). Subversive acts of revision: Writing and justice. *The English Journal, 102*(6), 31–39.

Dyches, J. (2018a). Investigating curricular injustices to uncover the injustices of curricula: Curriculum evaluation as critical disciplinary literacy practice. *The High School Journal, 101*(4), 236–250.

Dyches, J. (2018b). Shattering literary windows and mirrors: Creating prismatic canonical experiences for (and with) British literature students. In M. Macaluso & K. Macaluso (Eds.), *Teaching the canon in 21st century classrooms: Challenging genres* (pp. 35–49). Brill.

Freire, P. (2018). *Pedagogy of the oppressed.* Bloomsbury. (Original work published in 1970).

Freire, P., & Macedo, D. (1987). *Literacy: Reading the word and the world.* Bergin & Garvey.

Gee, J. P. (2015). *Social linguistics and literacies: Ideology in discourses* (5th ed.). Routledge.

Glaser, E. M. (1941). *An experiment in the development of critical thinking.* Teachers College.

hooks, b. (1994). *Teaching to transgress: Education as the practice of freedom.* Routledge.

Janks, H. (2005). Language and the design of texts. *English Teaching: Practice and Critique, 4*(3), 97–110.

Janks, H. (2012). The importance of critical literacy. *English Teaching: Practice and Critique, 11*(1), 150–163.

Kirkland, D. E. (2013). *A search past silence: The literacy of young Black men*. Teachers College Press.

Moje, E. B. (2015). Doing and teaching disciplinary literacy with adolescent learners: A social and cultural enterprise. *Harvard Educational Review, 85*(2), 254–278.

Morrell, E. (2005). Critical English education. *English Education, 37*(4), 312–321.

Morrell, E. (2008). *Critical literacy and urban youth: Pedagogies of access, dissent, and liberation*. Routledge.

Morrell, E. (2017). Toward equity and diversity in literacy research, policy, and practice: A critical, global approach. *Journal of Literacy Research, 49*(3), 454–463.

Paris, D. (2012). Culturally sustaining pedagogy: A needed change in stance, terminology, and practice. *Educational Researcher, 41*(3), 93–97.

Paris, D., & Alim, H. S. (2014). What are we seeking to sustain through culturally sustaining pedagogy? A loving critique forward. *Harvard Educational Review, 84*(1), 85–100.

Paris, D., & Alim, H. S. (Eds.). (2017). *Culturally sustaining pedagogies: Teaching and learning for justice in a changing world*. Teachers College Press.

Rainey, E. C. (2017). Disciplinary literacy in English language arts: Exploring the social and problem-based nature of literary reading and reasoning. *Reading and Research Quarterly, 52*(1), 53–71.

Sealey-Ruiz, Y. (2022). An archaeology of self for our times: Another talk to teachers. *English Journal, 111*(5), 21–26.

Scribner, S., & Cole, M. (1981). *The psychology of literacy*. Harvard University Press.

Street, B. V. (1984). *Literacy in theory and practice*. Cambridge University Press.

Street, B. V. (1994). What is meant by local literacies? *Language and Education*, 8(1–2), 9–17.

Sykes, E., & Hinger, S. (2021, May 14). *State lawmakers are trying to ban talk about race in schools*. ACLU. https://www.aclu.org/news/free-speech/state-lawmakers-are-trying-to-ban-talk-about-race-in-schools

2

What is Wobble?

If you are a current teacher or if you're studying to be a teacher and have created lesson plans and prepared to teach students, you have probably experienced wobble for one reason or another. The concept of wobble as it relates to teaching was identified and defined by Bob Fecho and colleagues Peg Graham and Sally Hudson-Ross more than 20 years ago (see Fecho et al., 2005). Since then, Fecho and colleagues have continued their scholarship on wobble (see Fecho et al., 2021), and other scholars have added to educators' understanding of wobble (see Garcia & O'Donnell-Allen, 2015). Before I provide their definition and research, I will share about a time I experienced wobble in my own teaching.

When I was teaching a grade 11 course, I wanted to teach the chapter titled "Speaking of Courage" from Tim O'Brien's (2009) *The Things They Carried*. In the chapter, Norman Bowker, after returning home from fighting in Vietnam, drives aimlessly in circles around a lake. At the conclusion of the chapter, the book includes O'Brien's notes on how he came to write "Speaking of Courage." Hoping to help my students understand the author's craft, I decided to have students read the notes as well.

I experienced wobble because, in the notes, O'Brien quotes a letter he received in 1975 from fellow soldier Norman Bowker. The letter contained some course language, including a term that sexualizes women. I questioned if this was appropriate to assign my students to read. Also, the chapter used the word *fuck*, and that is a curse word many find too offensive to encounter in school.

As I created my lesson plan, I experienced tension, doubt, and fear. I was afraid that if I went through with my plans to read the chapter along with the notes, parents or guardians would complain about the offensive language. I feared being summoned to the principal's office because of these imagined complaints. I was afraid too that some of my students, especially the young women in my class, would be offended when they read Bowker's letter. This tension, doubt, and fear are what wobble consists of. I wobbled when planning this lesson.

As I experienced wobble, I knew I needed to respond to that discomfort. First, I responded by justifying my decision to teach the chapter along with the notes. One thing that helped me justify my decision was that I had a class set of *The Things They Carried* provided by the textbook company the district had recently adopted. People above me had decided this book was acceptable to have in my classroom, so I determined it was fine if I used it in my teaching. Second, I asked students to read the notes at the conclusion of the chapter silently to themselves. I thought it would be best to handle any issues one-on-one to avoid inappropriate discussion or comments from other students. I remember walking around the class as students read silently, tensely waiting for a student to giggle or say something else inappropriate and hoping that no student would be too offended. I also hoped no student would complain to their parents or guardians about my lesson. Thankfully, nothing that I feared might happen did. My response to the wobble I felt allowed me to teach the text that caused me some tension, and my students were able to read an excellently written story and analyze the author's craft.

I didn't do anything during that lesson that I would consider critical literacy pedagogy (CLP), but my experience with wobble in this one lesson illustrates some of the main ideas of this chapter, which will address these questions: What is wobble? What can cause wobble? And why is wobble important?

What is Wobble?

As the word implies, Fecho et al.' (2005) concept of wobble concerns disequilibrium. They called wobble an "unsettling state of vertigo" (p. 175) that occurs when different forces, external and internal ones, push and pull on teachers. As Fecho et al. (2021) later explained, "This type of wobble isn't physical, but ideological and occurs in those moments where uncertainty presents itself and when possible directions for response don't readily come to questions that feel off center" (p. ix). When I experienced wobble because I was unsure about my lesson on O'Brien's book, I was uncertain if I was just being a prude or if Bowker's letter really was inappropriate. And the question of what is or isn't appropriate in school is an ideological one. My uncertainty caused discomfort for me in my teaching, and I had to respond to that discomfort as well as the questions it caused me to ask myself.

Fecho et al. (2021) explained that moments of wobble, or "moments of uncertainty and disequilibrium" (p. ix), can "often create circumstances in which understandings and realities may shift, within which teachers might feel a sense of dread, where the pedagogical ground underfoot will appear unstable" (p. ix). As my students read the notes to "Speaking of Courage," I experienced dread—dread over how they or their parents or guardians might respond and dread of getting in trouble with my administrators. That is why I decided to have students read the notes on their own; I had to respond to that dread somehow.

Teachers can experience wobble for lots of reasons. Daily, teachers must question their decisions as unexpected things occur in class, whether or not they are attempting to teach for CHANGE. Garcia and O'Donnell-Allen (2015) explained that wobble can occur for teachers "routinely" when

> something unexpected emerges, such as an unpredictable question that neither the students (nor you, for that matter) can adequately address, or a spat that breaks out between students that has absolutely nothing to do with the academic subject at hand.
>
> (p. 6)

They add that when teachers experience wobble, they "may feel as if nothing in [their] teacher education program has prepared [them] for [what they're encountering]" (p. 6). As you know, the teaching profession is full of unexpected moments—things that no professors or mentors could have known they would need to prepare us for. Wobble occurs quite naturally for educators. In this book, though, I want to focus on wobble that English language arts (ELA) teachers experience when they attempt to teach for CHANGE by providing CLP.

An important thing to remember about wobble is that each teacher experiences it uniquely. Something that can create wobble for me, in my teaching context, might not cause any wobble for you. Teaching contexts can vary drastically across the U.S., and so something that would be controversial for one teacher to teach might not be in a different context. Or something that one teacher wobbles about but is still considering teaching could be entirely out of the question for another teacher (see Fecho et al., 2005). When you experience wobble, please don't judge yourself if other teachers you know aren't experiencing that tension, dread, or doubt. Your wobble is yours, and you have every right to feel the way you do. Also, please respect other teachers' wobbles, even if they're wobbling over something that would not cause you any concern at all. Fecho et al. (2005) discovered there is value for teachers in recognizing what causes them to wobble and reflecting on the implications their wobble has for their teaching practice. Fecho (2011) described wobble as "a calling to attention, a provocation of response" (p. 6) to moments of discomfort and doubt. The wobble itself or what causes it is less important than how teachers decide to respond to it.

Garcia and O'Donnell-Allen (2015) used a metaphor to illustrate the value that paying attention to and responding to wobble can have for teachers. They compared the wobble that teachers encounter to the wobble that yoga practitioners experience. They explain that "practitioners of yoga assume particular 'poses' (e.g., tree, plank, warrior) designed to strengthen their bodies, lengthen muscles, improve balance, and increase mindfulness" (p. 3). For yoga practitioners to achieve their goals and progress in their practice, they have to practice their poses, and they "gradually add more difficult poses to their repertoire" (p. 3). Garcia and O'Donnell-Allen point out that yoga practitioners experience wobble as "a guaranteed and necessary part of the growth process" (p. 3), even though losing their balance and falling out of pose can be discouraging. In their metaphor, Garcia and O'Donnell-Allen compared teachers' approaches to teaching to poses that yoga practitioners attempt. From this perspective, teaching for CHANGE is a pose, an approach a teacher decides to attempt, and experiencing wobble, therefore, is part of their growth process. The yoga pose metaphor, however, might convey that teaching for CHANGE is something a teacher can try once and then abandon if it is too difficult (there are many yoga poses I'll never even attempt). For me, though, teaching for CHANGE by providing CLP is not something to try just once or implement only occasionally. It is a career-long commitment, and like practicing yoga, it requires lots of shaking, wobbling, and stretching. Deciding to provide CLP requires you to take on certain poses in your classroom. If you decide to assume those poses, you are guaranteed to wobble.

What Can Cause Wobble?

This chapter has already started to answer the question of what can cause wobble, and you have probably thought of some of your own experiences with wobble as you've been reading. In this section, I'll provide some answers with findings from my dissertation research, which I conducted during the 2021–2022 and 2022–2023 academic school years.

For my dissertation, I conducted a qualitative study of high school ELA teachers' experiences with and responses to wobble. Specifically, I wanted to understand how they wobbled regarding their implementation of CLP. Because I wanted to understand their experiences, my role was that of observer: I did not co-teach or co-plan any lessons. I also did not want and don't intend in this chapter to criticize or condemn the teachers who welcomed me into their classrooms. After receiving the necessary permissions, I began my study with ELA teachers. The teachers in the study all worked in the same school district located in the Southeastern region of the United States. Mrs. Skipmann and Ms. Wilson, both

teaching of feminist literary theories, Marxism, politicized issues, and racism
- Because they were not sure how certain students would respond during class discussions, and they wanted their classrooms to be safe spaces for all their students.

Of course, each of these teachers experienced these wobbles uniquely.

Mrs. Skipmann's Experiences with Wobble

Mrs. Skipmann was in her sixth year of teaching when the study began. The class I observed her teach was an English 3 Honors course, which is for students in grades 10 and 11 and focuses on American literature. Mrs. Skipmann was eager to provide CLP, especially because her juniors were close to voting age, and she wanted to help them become engaged citizens who contributed to making their communities better. As she attempted to provide CLP, though, she experienced lots of wobble.

Mrs. Skipmann wobbled, primarily because of fear: She feared losing her job if a parent or guardian complained about what occurred in her classroom, especially because of the increased scrutiny directed at teachers' classrooms in politically conservative states, like the one where my study took place. For example, after I observed a lesson during which Mrs. Skipmann facilitated a class discussion of a historical novel set in the 1880s that addressed racism, slavery, and the early American feminist movement in the U.S., I emailed Mrs. Skipmann and asked if there were any questions or issues she would have liked to address with students but did not because they were too "controversial." Mrs. Skipmann replied, "I didn't include any questions tying the book to today's world, but I think next time I would do so. It just felt a little too much for right now, particularly the way everything we do is scrutinized." In a different email, Mrs. Skipmann wrote, "I think there is so much public backlash from parents right now, and in general, that ends up being my biggest concern." When I interviewed Mrs. Skipmann again in the fall, she said, "Last year, it was like, 'This happened in Texas, this happened in Florida.' Now, it's like—shit. It's happening here."

White women, taught at Elliott High, and Mr. Tophi[l]
man, taught at Impavid High (all names are pseudony[r]
High served over 1,800 students and often outperform
the other high schools in the district where this study
(on ELA and mathematics standardized tests). Im[p]
served roughly 1,000 students and, compared with
the high schools in the district, usually underperforn[l]
standardized tests.

The data collection started with an initial intervi[e]
teacher. During the initial interviews, which I au
and transcribed, I asked them questions about thei[r]
ing of CLP and their experiences with wobble i[n]
ing. Then, in the spring of the 2021–2022 academ[ic]
I began classroom observations. With a few exce[pt]
of scheduling issues, I observed each teacher du
class period for three days a week for four cons
After these weeks of observations, I interviewe
again. Initially, this was going to be the end of my
I realized, though, that there was more to learn f[r]
ers, and they all graciously agreed to let me co[n]
semester (in the fall of the 2022–2023 school yea[r]
study. After the spring and fall semesters, I had
teacher four times and conducted at least 20 cl[a]
tions per teacher.

During classroom observations, I took
recorded what occurred in class. I transcribe
classroom recordings to focus on key mome[nts]
instruction or the teachers' interactions with t[he]
each observation, I emailed the teachers my l
Their emails and responses during intervi[ews]
understand their experiences with wobble i
After coding and analyzing the data, the fi[r]
these teachers wobbled, in general, for simi[lar]

- ♦ Because they were afraid of upsettin[g]
  ians if they studied "controversia[l]
  topics like abortion, genders, and s
- ♦ Because they feared the sociopolit[ical]
  ing their classrooms would cause [

Later in the same interview, she said, "[parents and guardians] are going to the board meetings. They're sharing stuff on [social media]. They're—your job could really be in question if you're doing the wrong thing right now. It's here."

During the first semester of observations, I asked Mrs. Skipmann if she intended to teach critical literary theories like feminism, Marxism, and postcolonialism.[1] She responded that she did not plan to teach them, in part, because "discussing some of these could cause some serious parent repercussions that I'm hesitant to be the kickstarter to." As discussed in Chapter 1, critical scholar Ernest Morrell (2008) encourages teachers to use these theories to engage their students in critical literacy. Mrs. Skipmann, though, did not feel supported enough by her school district to risk teaching these theories, for she quite understandably feared that she would face disciplinary action if a parent or guardian complained. This fear created wobble for Mrs. Skipmann that, during the first semester of my study, she did not think she could handle, so she did not teach those theories that semester.

When I returned to observe Mrs. Skipmann in the fall semester of the 2022–2023 school year, though, Mrs. Skipmann told me she had decided to teach feminism and Marxism with her new group of students. During an interview, I asked about her decision to teach these critical theories, even though doing so caused her to wobble. Reflecting on her decision, she said she realized that "I can do this. It's just a matter of will I do it?"

I was able to observe Mrs. Skipmann's first lesson on these theories. When Mrs. Skipmann projected the notes on Marxist literary theory on the board, her students immediately reacted:

GIA:	Oh my…
MISHA:	[Ironically imitating a conversation with a parent:] "What did you learn about today?"—"Marxism"
MRS. SKIPMANN:	There you go.
BEN:	[Addressing Mrs. Skipmann] Praying that you don't get any complaining emails [from parents].

As the students' comments demonstrate, they understood that the content of this lesson was something their parents or guardians might object to. When I emailed her about the wobble she experienced when teaching these theories, she wrote that these literary theories have "a stigma attached that have the potential to upset a parent." Thankfully, to the best of my knowledge, Mrs. Skipmann did not receive any "complaining emails" regarding her instruction.

Because of efforts to ban books written by or featuring characters who are members of LGBTQIA+ communities (see Limbong, 2022), Mrs. Skipmann also feared she would face disciplinary action if she included texts in her curriculum or classroom library that featured LGBTQIA+ characters or if she discussed sexuality in class. During one of the classroom observations in the spring, Mrs. Skipmann's class was studying chapter two of F. Scott Fitzgerald's *The Great Gatsby*. The chapter ends with Nick, the narrator who is assumed to be heterosexual, and another man drunkenly looking at photographs together in the man's bedroom. Mrs. Skipmann attempted to use this scene to challenge heteronormativity and to introduce a reading of the novel inspired by queer theory.[2] She said:

> So there's a couple different theories that I've heard as I've studied this particular section of the text.... It could be that, yes, Nick is gay and is in love with Gatsby. In fact, you could even read the novel the way.... And it could even be, yes, like, he could be gay. He could be bi[sexual].

Almost immediately after saying she heard *other* people interpret the novel this way, Mrs. Skipmann said, "Either way it doesn't really seem to affect the story at all.... Fitzgerald is basically taking a moment here to be like, 'It's not our business, it doesn't matter.'"

I interpreted Mrs. Skipmann's final comment on this question as evidence that discussing sexuality caused her to wobble, so I emailed her about it later that day. She responded,

> There's a huge focus politically right now on teachers discussing sexuality and I was nervous about getting

pushback from a parent on the discussion, but I know I have students who are gay and I want them to feel represented.

Her desire to support her students and to bring diverse perspectives into her curriculum often conflicted with the messages she and other teachers received from the school district and from state legislators where this study took place. This tension between her desire to support students and the surrounding political context created tension (i.e., wobble) for Mrs. Skipmann.

When I was collecting data, that state legislature was considering a few bills to limit classroom discourse on race, racism, and sexuality. One bill, if passed, would make it illegal for teachers to "advocate" for their LGBTQIA+ students. The district began requiring teachers to include a synopsis of every text they included in their course syllabi, and the district ELA specialist told the Elliott High English Department Chair, Ms. Wilson, to communicate to the other ELA teachers to be careful of the texts they included in their classroom libraries. Ironically, the district had purchased books for teachers' classroom libraries to increase the diversity of books available to students, but then district personnel told teachers they were each responsible for what books they had on their shelves. Mrs. Skipmann interpreted this warning to mean she should be careful about putting LGBTQIA+-inclusive texts on her shelves. This caused wobble and anger for Mrs. Skipmann, who said:

> But now they're telling us we have to go through and make sure there's nothing inappropriate in the books. Well, how do you define appropriate? What is appropriate? And also, why am I going to possibly be in trouble for these being on the shelf when you're the one who bought them? I did not pick these books. You provided them for me.... Help us! Don't just leave it on us.

The question "how do you define appropriate?" is one of tension, the tension between different perspectives and ideologies. Wobble occurs when conflicting ideologies collide.

In my final interview with Mrs. Skipmann, I asked her if she thought she might teach queer theory in the future along with other critical literary theories. She responded:

> That's where I think it gets scary. Because I think, morally, nobody can argue that women don't deserve rights.... But I feel like when you touch queer theory, there are so many people that get angry about it. It's something I would like to do, because I have LGBTQ students in every class.... They're reading it through a queer lens already.... I'm open to it. I just think I'd want to prepare. Like, cover my butt more. Because like I said, they're already doing it, and I think they deserve to have representation. But it also scares me.

In the state where this study took place, teaching queer theory was not the norm. In fact, Mrs. Skipmann said that, in her teacher education program, none of her courses prepared her to provide CLP or to teach queer theory.

Mrs. Skipmann also wobbled on top of wobbling. When I asked her in an interview in May 2022 what the consequences were for her as a human and a teacher that she felt she had to "play it safe," as she said, in her teaching, she responded:

> Yeah. I mean, it stinks. I get scared that, you know, the wrong person's going to go to their parent. That parent's going to contact [school administrators], and then I'm going to get in trouble. And then I feel like I'm not supporting them enough. You know, especially, like currently we have the *Roe vs. Wade* going on, and I've heard female students discussing it. And I want to jump in there and have that conversation with them and let them know that [I support them], but ... I can't do that. And I hate it so much. Like, it's one of my least favorite parts of my job is that I can't do more with [critical literacy pedagogy].

When Mrs. Skipmann shared this with me, I felt her frustration and desperation. As I interpreted this comment, the tension between keeping her job and doing her best to support her students created a supra-wobble for Mrs. Skipmann: She felt that by not upsetting parents/guardians, she was not supporting her students enough, and this created additional wobble for her. She wanted to be able to enact CLP to support her students who were wrestling with real-world issues that impacted their lives, but the wobble she experienced and the messaging she received from the school district, state legislators, and some parents/guardians in her community made her feel she could lose her job if she pursued critical literacy too overtly.

In that same interview, I asked Mrs. Skipmann what the consequences were for her students that she sometimes had to self-censor her teaching and limit her goals for instruction. She responded:

> They don't know that I'm an advocate. They don't know that I'm there for them. They don't know that I'm a safe space—that if they're struggling they can come to and talk to me. And that's what you lose when you have this tightening up of what teachers can and can't say.

Based on my observations, I believe Mrs. Skipmann's students actually did know she was there for them, and I believe they did see her classroom as a safe space. Still, Mrs. Skipmann felt she was not doing enough for her students because of the restrictive environment she worked in and the wobbles that teaching in such a context caused.

Mrs. Skipmann wobbled when she felt that providing CLP could get her in trouble, especially because she doubted she would be supported by the school district, which had recently sided with a parent who complained about texts in an Advanced Placement language and composition course at a different school. Mrs. Skipmann's desire to provide CLP also conflicted with her needs as a human. She needed, and deserved, to be supported by her school district and to feel safe while performing her job. Mrs. Skipmann deserved to be treated with respect, but the sociopolitical discourse surrounding teaching in the past several years has been anything but respectful toward educators (see Hines & Penn, 2023). When her beliefs conflicted with the restrictions imposed on her and her teaching, Mrs. Skipmann wobbled. She experienced doubt, dread, and fear as she was unsure of how to respond to the tension she encountered.

Ms. Wilson's Experiences with Wobble

When the study began, Ms. Wilson was in her 20th year of teaching and was the English department chair at Elliott High. The class I observed her teach was an English 2 Honors course. This course is for students in grades 9 and 10 and focuses on world literature.

Ms. Wilson wobbled because she too feared upsetting students' parents or guardians. In the first interview, Ms. Wilson said, "I feel like we're being closely watched. I feel like I have to be careful about what I say, what we read, what's on my shelf. And I've never really overly worried about stuff like that before." As we discussed why Ms. Wilson felt she needed to be more careful now than in the past, she told me about the experience of another ELA teacher at Elliott High:

> [They] had a student last year when we were doing the Cultural Conflicts essay,[3] and a parent got all up in arms.... And I think [rights for transgender people] was one of the options. Anyway, the parent called and would email and was like, "You're trying to push this on my kid.".... It was just one of the options. But the parent gave [the teacher] a really hard time about that. And that's the kind of stuff that you don't want.... You want to be careful about what you say.... If a parent gets wind of something and misconstrues it, then you have a whole other level you have to deal with.

It is important to note that teachers can, like Ms. Wilson did, experience wobble because of something that happened to another teacher they know.

In the same interview, I asked Ms. Wilson about opportunities for CLP with her world literature curriculum. In previous years, Ms. Wilson taught Athol Fugard's play *"Master Harold" ... and the Boys*, which takes place in the 1950s in South African during Apartheid and includes moments of racism and uses racist slurs. She said she was not going to teach it anymore because the previous semester a student read a racial slur out loud, even though Ms. Wilson had instructed students not to, and this incident created a lot of conflict amongst the students. I asked when she taught the play in the past if she used it as a tool to challenge racism that continues to take place today, and she said, "So, I did not go into specifics…. Nothing deep. Nothing deep. Because, again, I'm fearful of what I say."

When Ms. Wilson thought about addressing issues of race and racism occurring today in the U.S., she wobbled, for she feared that a student's parents or guardians would complain. This fear is understandable because there has been a national outcry against "teaching Critical Race Theory" (CRT). CRT is an academic framework that unpacks how the legal system in the United States creates and supports inequitable and oppressive structures in everyday society (Delgado & Stefancic, 2017). While CRT is not part of official high school curricula, it may influence a teacher's instruction, and some teachers have been accused of "teaching CRT" if they lead class discussions on race and racism that emphasize racism's persistence in society (see Natanson & Balingit, 2022; Stout & Wilburn, 2022). I asked Ms. Wilson if she was afraid about being accused of "teaching CRT," and she said that was one of her concerns.

Like Mrs. Skipmann, Ms. Wilson was aware of book-banning efforts targeting books featuring LGBTQIA+ characters. As previously mentioned, before I began my study, the school district purchased books for ELA teachers' classroom libraries. The message teachers received from the district ELA specialist communicated that they would not be supported by the district if a parent or guardian complained about a book on their shelf, even if the district purchased it. This caused wobble for both Mrs. Skipmann and Ms. Wilson.

In the first interview, Ms. Wilson pointed to a stack of boxes containing the new books the district purchased. She said, "there seems to be more controversy with books and banned books." And added, "the district pushed those books, but no one's read all those books. I don't want to put a book on my shelf that I don't know what it is. So that's why they're sitting in boxes right now." By the conclusion of my study, Ms. Wilson had unpacked and perused the books. She put most of them on her classroom shelves, but she kept three books in her back closet, away from students. Two of these books featured LGBTQIA+ characters, and one addressed teen suicide. Ms. Wilson feared she would not be supported by the district if a parent or guardian complained about these texts. This created tension for her that she had to respond to, for all wobbles demand our attention and require us to "determine mindfully how to respond" (Garcia & O'Donnell-Allen, 2015, p. 9). Ms. Wilson responded to the wobble these books caused by keeping some—the ones she thought had the most potential for provoking a parent or guardian complaint—tucked away in the closet.

Mr. Tophill's Experiences with Wobble

Mr. Tophill, who taught at a different high school from Mrs. Skipmann and Ms. Wilson, was in his second year of teaching when the study began. The class I observed him teach was English 4 College Prep (CP), a course for seniors who were not tracked in the gifted-and-talented program. English 4 CP, according to the district expectations, is supposed to focus on British literature, but Mr. Tophill said, "I don't think our students are learning what they need to learn through British Lit." He stressed that most of his students spoke Spanish at home and that their lives were far removed from the contexts and storylines of the literature often included in traditional British literature curricula. He did teach the epic poem *Beowulf* and a few other texts usually covered in English 4 CP, but I never observed him teaching British literature.

In an interview, we discussed his decision to disrupt the traditional approach to teaching English 4 CP, and Mr. Tophill emphasized that, in addition to trying to make his teaching more relevant for his students, being a person of color was a motivating factor. He wanted to disrupt "the fact that the literature we read in English classes is usually White male-centered." Mr. Tophill's teaching was not aligned with the district's expectations, and while I imagine that teaching against the status quo in similar ways could cause wobble for many teachers, interestingly, Mr. Tophill said he did not feel any wobble regarding this decision.

Mr. Tophill did experience wobble for other reasons. Unlike Mrs. Skipmann and Ms. Wilson, though, Mr. Tophill's wobbles occurred mostly because of fears related to his students, not their parents or guardians. Because he taught seniors, and many of them were legal adults who worked jobs outside of school and yearned to be treated as adults, this makes sense. Mr. Tophill's students were more likely to say something directly to him than to complain to their parents or guardians.

One way Mr. Tophill tried to disrupt the traditional, "White male-centered" British literary canon was by teaching feminist literary theory. From the very beginning of my study, Mr. Tophill taught this theory and Marxist literary theory. But Mr. Tophill said that, of these two, feminism was "the hardest" to teach because of student resistance and pushback. In an interview, Mr. Tophill imitated his students, saying, "I don't like it. I think it's stupid. I don't want to be a feminist."

In the second semester of observations, I got to see some of this resistance occur in his classroom. During a lesson, Mr. Tophill placed students in groups to read about and discuss different critical literary theories. One of the groups assigned to discuss feminism started talking with raised voices because a young man in the group, Tyrese, said something that a young woman, Aisha, objected to. Mr. Tophill walked over to ease the tension:

MR. TOPHILL: [Clarifying for Aisha what Tyrese said] No, he said, "Boys can't be feminists." Do you think you're a feminist?
TYRESE: No!
MR. TOPHILL: Why?
TYRESE: [As a man,] I can't say that—
MR. TOPHILL: No, no. *Feminist* and *feminine* are two different things.... We're not trying to make y'all feminist. But to be smart means to be able to look at this from a different point of view and keep your point of view. So even if you don't believe in the feminist movement—The point is not that you be a feminist. The point is that you understand what does feminism say.
TYRESE: Oh, okay, then....

Mr. Tophill and I discussed this kind of resistance from students. I asked him if the potential for student pushback caused wobble for him, and Mr. Tophill said, "Of course. Because what I don't want is somebody says something inappropriate because I'm going to have to address it." He added, "and sometimes those conversations can be volatile. Sometimes those conversations can be problematic." In a different interview, Mr. Tophill said, "Navigating feminist theory has been very hard for me because I have to make sure that I'm teaching these students who—if we're being honest, are misogynists—with passion." Mr. Tophill's wobbles were primarily caused because he feared how his students might respond and what harmful, problematic statements they might make if they resisted his instruction.

When Mr. Tophill taught Marxism, though, he did not experience wobble. I watched him teach several lessons on this theory and never observed any pushback from students. In an interview, Mr. Tophill explained why teaching Marxism was not that challenging for him:

> Marxism, however, is the easiest to teach because our kids are very critical of the economy. They're very critical of money and how money is used. Most of our kids have jobs. Most of our kids get out at [noon] and go to work.... So, they understand.

It was fascinating to see that Mrs. Skipmann's students recognized that teaching Marxism had the potential of getting Mrs. Skipmann in trouble, while teaching Marxism caused no issues for Mr. Tophill, though he taught in the same school district and city as Mrs. Skipmann. For him, it was the reverse: Teaching feminism, but not Marxism, was challenging. This is an excellent example of how wobble is unique to each teacher: Teachers wobble for different reasons, depending on their teaching contexts and students. This is also why educators should not judge each other or themselves for the wobbles we experience. If you are the only one in your department experiencing a specific wobble, that is okay!

Just like Mrs. Skipmann, though, Mr. Tophill experienced wobble when contemplating teaching queer theory. Again, teaching queer theory was not the norm in the district in which Mrs. Skipmann and Mr. Tophill taught, and Mr. Tophill too doubted the support he could expect to receive if he tried to teach it. Not only did Mr. Tophill doubt the support he would receive from the school district if a student or parent/guardian complained, but he also doubted the support he could expect to receive from his own administrators. In an interview, he told me it was rumored that before he was hired his principal shut down Impavid High's Genders and Sexualities Alliance (GSA Network, n.d.) club. In the same interview, Mr. Tophill said, "I want to make sure that my queer students are safe in that atmosphere [when studying queer theory]. And I don't know if [Impavid High School] is there right now."

In addition to fearing a lack of support if he taught queer theory, Mr. Tophill wobbled because he feared how his students would react and what problematic, homophobic things they might say. When we discussed this tension in an interview, Mr. Tophill said:

> And I just would hate for us to be in here talking about queer theory, and there's a queer kid sitting here, and having to do see that their classmates truly don't like them because of their identity. I don't feel like enough kids would come forward and truly be on their side and help them through it.... I think that's really what keeps me from going that route is because I don't know what's going to happen. I may bring it up, and everything is fine, I may bring it up, and all hell breaks loose. I just simply don't know, and I don't know if I'm ready to gamble with that possibility yet.

Mr. Tophill wobbled because how his students might react to his instruction on queer theory was unpredictable, and he was not sure he could provide a safe space for his students who were members of LGBTQIA+ communities.

In my final interview with him, Mr. Tophill shared another reason that caused him to wobble when he contemplated teaching queer theory:

> [Challenging students' views is] inherently violent, it just is. Taking students out of their comfort zone and exposing them to a new ideology is essentially like chipping away at their old ideology, and kids are going to fight to hold on to that. Sometimes they let it go, and sometimes they keep holding on to it. But I think that's one of the key things that I had to think about. You know, am I ready to violently shake these kids out of their mold?.... So do I think I'm ready to do that? I don't think so.

Mr. Tophill questioned if he believed it was right for him to "violently shake" his students from their previous ways of viewing the world. I see this conflict as an internal one that Mr. Tophill will obviously need to reflect on for himself.

All teachers must reflect on the wobbles created from internal conflicts so they can make mindful decisions in their teaching. In the same interview, Mr. Tophill said, "I also need to make sure that I'm ready for the fight that comes with teaching a certain ideology that needs to be taught, but also, that is going to be inherently violent for these students." Before he could teach queer theory, Mr. Tophill felt he needed to spend some time preparing for the kinds of conflicts, internal and external, such instruction could create. In an earlier interview, offering advice to teachers contemplating implementing CLP, Mr. Tophill said, "if you're not ready yourself—don't. Because you'll do more harm than good."

Why is Wobble Important?

Fecho et al. (2005) argued that when educators pay attention to their wobbles, they have "opportunities for examining [their teaching] practice in ways that might not otherwise occur" (p. 175). Fecho (2011) wrote, "wobble taps us on the shoulder and induces us to ask why" (p. 53). When you experience wobble caused from teaching for CHANGE, ask yourself why. Understanding why you're wobbling can help you look deeper into your teaching context, your beliefs and teaching philosophy, and your needs as a human and professional. Once you've discovered the *why* behind a wobble, you're ready to act to address your needs with a level of insight and renewed commitment you probably would not have obtained without wobbling in the first place. Wobble is important because paying attention to and responding to it are excellent ways for teachers to grow in their teaching practice.

Remember Garcia and O'Donnell-Allen's (2015) yoga metaphor? For a yoga practitioner to progress in accomplishing more and more challenging poses, or to improve the ones they can already perform, they must wobble—they must endure frustration and discomfort. Wobble, for a yoga practitioner, "signals a commitment to increased discipline and deepened practice" (Garcia & O'Donnell-Allen, p. 3). Of course, yoga practitioners also know not to push their bodies too much too quickly. They are aware of their current limitations and little by little stretch themselves and strengthen their muscles to progress in their yoga practice. As they continue to deepen their practice in ways they and their bodies can handle, they eventually can take on poses that were previously impossible. Fecho (2011) wrote, "where there is wobble, change is occurring" (p. 53). When you wobble in your teaching practice, you too can grow so that, in time, you can accomplish exciting things with your students in your teaching that you previously never imagined being comfortable enough to pursue.

If you decide to commit to providing CLP in your teaching, you will wobble. The encouraging thing is that your wobble is a sign of your increased discipline and dedication to your students and to improving, deepening, and expanding your teaching practice. Garcia and O'Donnell-Allen (2015) put it this way: "When you wobble, it doesn't mean that you're failing. Rather it signals that you are pursuing worthwhile poses that require learning, reflection, and professional growth" (p. 6). I imagine you have experienced the value of reflection in your own teaching practice: Reflection allows teachers to take action to improve their teaching and experience professional growth. In his book on what he called "optimal" human experience, the late professor Mihaly Csikszentmihalyi (1990) explained the importance of action coupled with reflection:

> Activity and reflection should ideally complement and support each other. Action by itself is blind, reflection impotent. Before investing great amounts of energy in a goal, it pays to raise the fundamental questions: Is this something I really want to do? Is it something I enjoy doing? Am I likely to enjoy it in the foreseeable future? Is the price that I—and others—will have to pay worth it? Will I be able to live with myself if I accomplish it?
>
> (p. 226)

Wobble is important because it forces us to pause and pay attention. When we pay attention to wobble, we are compelled to reflect, which can "complement and support" our activity in our classrooms.

Mrs. Skipmann and Mr. Tophill's experiences with wobble illustrate some of these points. Mrs. Skipmann grew in her teaching, at least in part, because she wobbled when contemplating teaching critical literary theories. Her wobble caused her to pause and ponder why. After she reflected on her wobble, she realized she could be brave, and she put that bravery into action when she taught her students feminism and Marxism and helped them use those approaches to studying literature as tools to critique abuses of power and injustices. Mr. Tophill's wobble helped him realize the internal work he needed to pursue if he were to teach queer theory. Mr. Tophill knew his own limits, and he did not push himself beyond them before he was ready.

Paying attention to and responding wisely to wobble are important because it can help you know your own limits so you don't implement CLP in ways that produce reactions or consequences you're completely unprepared for. If you're not prepared for potential ramifications of teaching for CHANGE by implementing CLP, at this very moment, that is okay. It is better to know that now than to do something in class with your students that exposes you and them to controversy and harm.

As you continue to read this book, please don't feel pressured to provide CLP in ways you're currently not prepared for or don't have the needed supports from colleagues, administrators, or your school district to perform. I do encourage you, though, to embrace moments of wobble, no matter how uncomfortable they are, instead of ignoring them. Embracing moments of wobble will help you increase your stretchiness for future wobbles, which is the subject of the next chapter.

Notes

1 In Chapters 6 and 7, I define and explain how teachers can use these critical theories to provide CLP.
2 Queer theory "questions the fixed categories of sexual identity" and rejects "normative (that is, what is considered 'normal') sexual ideology" that views heterosexuality as the only acceptable sexuality (Brewton, n.d., para 27).
3 For this essay, Ms. Wilson explained that students chose topics to research and write about.

References

Brewton, V. (n.d.). *Literary theory*. Internet Encyclopedia of Philosophy. https://iep.utm.edu/literary/#H8

Csikszentmihalyi, M. (1990). *Flow: The psychology of optimal experience*. Harper & Row.

Delgado, R., & Stefancic, J. (2017). *Critical race theory: An introduction* (3rd ed.). NYU Press.

Fecho, B. (2011). *Teaching for the students: Habits of heart, mind, and practice in the engaged classroom*. Teachers College Press.

Fecho, B., Graham, P., & Hudson-Ross, S. (2005). Appreciating the wobble: Teacher research, professional development, and figured worlds. *English Education, 37*(3), 174–199.

Fecho, B., Coombs, D., Stewart, T. T., & Hawley, T. (2021). *Novice teachers embracing wobble in standardized schools: Using dialogue and inquiry for self-reflection and growth*. Routledge.

Garcia, A., & O'Donnell-Allen, C. (2015). *Pose, wobble, flow: A culturally proactive approach to literacy instruction*. Teachers College Press.

GSA Network. (n.d.). *What is a GSA club?* https://gsanetwork.org/what-is-a-gsa/

Hines, C. M., & Penn, J. I. (2023). Seeing beyond the surface: Using critical lenses to combat anti-Blackness in the English classroom. *English Journal, 113*(1), 17–24.

Limbong, A. (2022, September 19). *New report finds a coordinated rise in attempted book bans*. NPR. https://www.npr.org/2022/09/19/1123156201/new-report-finds-a-coordinated-rise-in-attempted-book-bans

Morrell, E. (2008). *Critical literacy and urban youth: Pedagogies of access, dissent, and liberation*. Routledge.

Natanson, H., & Balingit, M. (2022, June 16). *Caught in the culture wars, teachers are being forced from their jobs*. The Washington Post. https://www.washingtonpost.com/education/2022/06/16/teacher-resignations-firings-culture-wars/

Stout, C., & Wilburn, T. (2022, February 1). *CRT Map: Efforts to restrict teaching racism and bias have multiplied across the U.S.* Chalkbeat. https://www.chalkbeat.org/22525983/map-critical-race-theory-legislation-teaching-racism/

Literature Cited

O'Brien, T. (2009). *The things they carried*. Mariner Classics.

3

What is *Stretchiness?*

I'm not flexible at all. I can't fold over my legs and touch my toes. I'm lucky if I can reach slightly above my ankle. I also don't have good balance. In short, I'm not proficient with yoga poses that require balance and flexibility—so, most of them. I still enjoy practicing yoga, though. When I practice yoga, I struggle to maintain the poses I'm trying to perform. Instead of touching my toes, I touch above my ankle and embrace the discomfort caused from the tightness in my muscles. When the instructor asks me to perform tree pose—which requires me to stand on one leg, leg locked straight, and to rest the bottom of my other foot on the inner thigh of my standing leg—I rest my foot on my calf because that's easier for me. I can do the pose that way for about 10 seconds before I lose my balance and drop both feet to the ground. When this happens, I breathe and start again. Currently, I can't perform tree pose with my foot resting on the inner thigh of my standing foot. I know, though, that in time, my balance will improve as the needed muscles will strengthen and I gain the required flexibility. I embrace the wobble now, hoping that in the future I'll be able to perform the pose better, and I know that if I get upset or too discouraged, I'm entirely missing the point of practicing yoga.

This chapter returns to Garcia and O'Donnell-Allen's (2015) yoga metaphor. As discussed in the previous chapter, they applied Fecho et al.' (2005) concept of wobble (i.e., tensions, doubt, and dread that teachers experience) to yoga practice. Garcia and O'Donnell-Allen compared yoga poses to approaches that teachers adopt to guide their instruction. In this book, the pose I'm writing about is the decision to teach for CHANGE by implementing critical literacy pedagogy (CLP). Garcia and O'Donnell-Allen explained that when teachers adopt a pose, they will likely experience a repeating cycle of posing, wobbling, and growing professionally by responding to wobble and improving in their teaching practice—and then wobbling all over again. They call this the Pose, Wobble, Flow (P/W/F) framework.

Garcia and O'Donnell-Allen (2015) used Csikszentmihalyi's (1990) concept of *flow* in their P/W/F framework. As Csikszentmihalyi explained, flow includes "the positive aspects of human experience–joy, creativity, the process of total involvement with life" (p. xi). For Csikszentmihalyi, moments of flow are "the best moments in our lives" (p. 3), but he argued they rarely occur during relaxing times, when we might expect to be living our best life. Instead, Csikszentmihalyi stated, "the best moments usually occur when a person's body or mind is stretched to its limits in a voluntary effort to accomplish something difficult and worthwhile" (p. 3). Csikszentmihalyi pointed out that achieving "optimal experience is thus something that we *make* happen" (p. 3). Citing Csikszentmihalyi in their P/W/F framework, Garcia and O'Donnell-Allen argue that "individuals become more capable and skilled as a result of the flow experience" (p. 7).

When I'm struggling to perform tree pose and shaking and hopping around on my yoga mat, I can experience flow, even though I'm having to battle my poor balance and frustration. That's why I still enjoy practicing yoga. Of course, my yoga practice is not nearly as important to me as my career as an educator. I imagine that, in your teaching career, you've experienced flow, too. Your first year of teaching, like mine, probably afforded you lots of opportunities to take on a challenge that stretched you to your limits. I bet that, as you overcame those challenges, you experienced that exhilaration Csikszentmihalyi wrote about. I bet that, wherever you are in your teaching career now, each year presents you with challenges that you continue to overcome.

With each new challenge you overcome, you've probably realized that you can make optimal experiences happen in your classroom—you can achieve flow.

The concept of flow, then, is closely related to the concept of wobble. When we wobble as educators, we experience tension, doubt, and dread that can create challenges for us. We can find ourselves stretched to our limits. To grow and improve in our teaching practice, though, we must respond to that wobble somehow. The concept of flow encourages me as an educator. Flow shows me that making intentional actions to address the wobble I experience can allow me to enjoy experiencing that wobble, even though wobbling can be frightening and uncomfortable. The concept of flow encourages me to expand my stretchiness for wobble.

What is *Stretchiness?*

Just as Garcia and O'Donnell-Allen (2015) did in their book *Pose, Wobble, Flow: A Culturally Proactive Approach to Literacy Instruction*, in this chapter I use Csikszentmihalyi's (1990) concept of flow to expand on Fecho et al.'s (2005) concept of wobble and to extend the wobble-yoga metaphor. The study I conducted for my dissertation and this book are indebted to the work of these scholars. As I analyzed the data I collected (see Chapter 2), though, I realized my study's findings had additional insights into wobble, and these insights helped me conceptualize what I call *stretchiness*. Fecho (2011) reflected that "by taking advantage of difficulties we encounter and stretching our tolerances for wobble [...] we can come to appreciate those very forces that now might appear discomforting" (p. 35). Csikszentmihalyi argued that flow occurs when people intentionally stretch themselves to their limits as they pursue something they find meaningful and worth the discomfort. As the yoga metaphor demonstrates, when people wobble and work through the cycle of posing, wobbling, and obtaining flow, they can stretch themselves beyond what they thought their limits were to achieve personal and professional growth. As Fecho et al. (2005) originally recognized, paying attention to and responding to wobble can help teachers grow in their teaching practice "in ways that might not otherwise occur" (p. 175). The concept of stretchiness expands on the original conception of wobble, though, because it recognizes that there are consequences for a teacher's practice depending on the ways they respond to wobble: Some responses to wobble produce more professional growth than others.

Since this book focuses on teaching for CHANGE by providing CLP, my concept of *stretchiness* does too. As I see it, *stretchiness* is a teacher's current readiness and commitment to teaching for CHANGE despite the wobbles they encounter. You can also think of it as their preparedness for wobble they will encounter when providing CLP. This concept recognizes that, just as with physical muscles, people can expand their stretchiness. If, like Mrs. Skipmann was, you're currently experiencing too much wobble to try to teach students critical literary theories like feminism and Marxism, this does not mean you will never be able to teach them. It is possible that you, just like Mrs. Skipmann, will expand your stretchiness for wobble and adopt CLP "poses" that you previously never imagined being able to perform. Your current level of stretchiness does not mean you should be discouraged or look down on yourself. Your stretchiness can expand over time, allowing you to be more and more comfortable teaching for CHANGE in ways that you previously could not imagine doing. For that to happen, though, you'll need to remind yourself that achieving flow—those exhilarating experiences that can give tremendous meaning to your life—is possible precisely because of the things causing you doubt, tension, and dread, and you will need to respond productively to wobbles you experience. When you expand your stretchiness by responding productively to wobble, those moments that caused you dread can help you enjoy your teaching more than if you never wobbled.

The concept of stretchiness extends Garcia and O'Donnell-Allen's yoga metaphor: When teachers' stretchiness for wobble is expanded (i.e., when metaphorically their flexibility and strength needed to perform a pose increase), teachers can deepen their poses—that is, they can stretch themselves to endure wobble and continue teaching for CHANGE. When teachers' stretchiness for wobble is restricted, or their metaphorical muscles become tightened up, teachers will drop out of the pose (i.e., they will stop enacting CLP). Because stretchiness can impact a teacher's ability to teach for CHANGE, it is crucial to understand what impacts or affects stretchiness. Of course, just like wobble, each person's stretchiness is unique to them, but as I analyzed the data I collected with Mrs. Skipmann, Ms. Wilson, and Mr. Tophill, I discovered some factors that can impact a teacher's stretchiness.

What Can Affect a Teacher's Stretchiness?

The general answer to this question is that how teachers respond to their wobbles affects their stretchiness. If teachers respond to their wobbles by choosing to accept the discomfort, respond to it intentionally, and remain committed to providing CLP, they will act in ways that push themselves to expand their stretchiness. If, however, they respond to wobble by allowing it to take away their agency and to dominate what they say and do in the classroom, their stretchiness will become (or remain) restricted. I write this as an observation, not as a judgment. I don't mean to condemn any teacher for wishing to avoid wobble and for restricting their stretchiness. Many times in my teaching, I have chosen to alter my lesson plans or goals for my instruction so that I could avoid wobble. I also should recognize that many teachers, especially minoritized, racialized, and otherwise discriminated against teachers, might put their jobs, health, and safety at risk if they teach for CHANGE by enacting CLP. Again, this book is meant to encourage you in your teaching practice, not censure you. It is important, though, to be aware of how your wobbles and your responses to them affect your stretchiness.

Wobbles occur amongst tensions and conflicts between different forces surrounding teachers. In my study, some of the larger forces surrounding the teachers' classrooms that caused them to wobble were school district policies or official communications sent to teachers; restrictive state laws or bills that attempted to punish teachers for providing CLP; unfavorable discourse surrounding the teaching profession expressed in the news and on social media; and examples of how other English language arts (ELA) teachers in the country, school district, or even their own schools were punished because of parent or guardian complaints. In the previous chapter, I discussed the wobbles that Mrs. Skipmann, Ms. Wilson, and Mr. Tophill experienced. In this chapter, I want to return to their wobbles and provide examples of how their responses to those moments of discomfort affected their stretchiness. When I analyzed the data, I discovered that how they responded to their wobbles could either restrict or expand their stretchiness.

What Restricts Stretchiness?

Stretchiness is a teacher's readiness to enact CLP, and when they wobble, stretchiness includes their commitment to CLP despite the wobbles they experience. A teacher's stretchiness fluctuates because it is based on their responses to wobble. Your current stretchiness can change by tomorrow's lesson. Your current stretchiness can expand, allowing you to endure more and more discomfort as you remain committed to teaching for CHANGE. It could become restricted, depending on how you respond to your wobbles, though, which will make it more difficult for you to enact CLP. Certain factors may cause a teacher to respond to wobble in ways that reduce their stretchiness. In my research, I found that teachers' perceptions of their students as well as their teaching contexts caused them to respond to wobbles by being careful with their word choices, by limiting their goals for the CLP they provided, and by practicing self-censorship. These responses restricted their stretchiness.

Teachers' Perceptions of Their Students

When Mrs. Skipmann experienced wobble because of her assumptions about her students, she occasionally responded in ways that restricted her stretchiness. In an interview, Mrs. Skipmann said:

> I have students who are very much on this side [on a "controversial" issue], and they'll tell you they're on this side. And I have students who are on [an opposing] side, and they're sitting next to each other. And I don't want to start a huge uproar, so I have to be careful.

Her awareness of the students' conflicting viewpoints caused her to wobble, and sometimes she responded to that wobble by being careful about what kinds of discussions or class activities she chose to pursue. For example, in the first semester of observations, Mrs. Skipmann and her students studied excerpts of Henry David Thoreau's writings. Mrs. Skipmann's students started making connections to politics in the world today. One of her students, Charles, a young man who is gay, mentioned Florida's "Don't Say Gay Bill" (see Diaz, 2022). Charles said, "[Politicians] don't know how bills like that will affect people." In the politically and religiously conservative state where this study took place, Mrs. Skipmann undoubtedly knew Charles's comment could start an "uproar." Perhaps that is why she quickly followed Charles's statement by saying:

> It's kind of like we elect these people to be our voice, but then they don't always do that. They kind of are their own voice, I feel like. That's just my opinion. And not every official is that way. I'm not trying to state a political opinion. I'm stating, like, how I see things.

Mrs. Skipmann's comment seems like an attempt to move away from a specific critique, especially one regarding rights for LGBTQIA+ people that not all her students would agree with, to a more general critique that most students could accept. Interestingly, when she did that, she experienced wobble because she feared being accused of stating a "political opinion." After this observation, I emailed her about this class discussion and asked if she experienced wobble. She wrote:

> Oh definitely. I was trying really hard to not let my political opinions show as I listened and took in all of their comments. I handled it by trying to be careful with my words and stick [sic] with facts instead of opinions as I spoke.

When Mrs. Skipmann responded by being careful, her stretchiness was restricted, and the class did not get to pursue important, relevant topics as deeply as they could have.

Mr. Tophill's stretchiness for wobble, too, was impacted by his perceptions of his students. As mentioned in the previous chapter, Mr. Tophill believed his students were "misogynists," and he told me that teaching feminist literary theory was "the hardest" because his students pushed back against many of the tenets of feminism. His perception of his students created some wobble for him, mainly because he was afraid they would say something problematic or harmful in class. He responded to this wobble by limiting the goals for his instruction on feminism. As he told his student Tyrese, "The point is not that you be a feminist. The point is that you understand what does feminism say." A few days later, Mr. Tophill's students applied some of the tenets of feminism when they read a short story, told in the first person, from the perspective of a man who stalks a woman in a subway. Mr. Tophill and his students discussed the problematic ways the stalker described the woman's body and clothes, and they interrogated the power differentials in the story between the man and the woman he was stalking.

Feminist literary theory, though, encourages readers to resist patriarchal systems that oppress women (Dobie, 2009). As I observed students discussing the short story about the stalker, I felt that this text did not push against the patriarchy much, if at all. This short story seemed like it fit Mr. Tophill's goal of helping his students "understand what does feminism say," but the instruction did not push students to work toward critiquing or dismantling the patriarchy. I emailed Mr. Tophill and asked him to reflect on his teaching of this theory. He responded, "I think students understand Feminist Theory on a base level. I do not feel like I was able to challenge them with the literary theory as much as I would have liked." Mr. Tophill responded to the wobble caused by teaching this critical theory by limiting his goals for his instruction, which restricted his stretchiness for this specific discomfort. His response resulted in students having fewer opportunities to engage with feminist literary theory on a deeper level.

Teachers' Experiences in Their Teaching Contexts

The three teachers in the study wobbled because of larger forces impacting their teaching contexts. For example, as discussed in the previous chapter, Mrs. Skipmann and Ms. Wilson both wobbled when the school district's ELA specialist warned that each teacher was responsible for the books in their classroom libraries. They interpreted this to mean that the district would not support them if a parent or guardian complained about a book in their classroom library, even if the district purchased the text in question. Complaints about books in teachers' classroom libraries and book-banning efforts make national news and are an excellent example of outside forces impacting secondary ELA teachers' classroom decisions. Ms. Wilson responded to this wobble by self-censoring the texts she placed in her classroom library. Speaking of the books she tucked away from students in her back closet, Ms. Wilson said:

> I went and talked to [the media center specialist] about them. And both of these [books] she said were questioned but she has them both in the [school] library....but I just wanted to read them, and I just haven't had a chance to do that, so I just kept them in the back.

The school district's ELA specialist did not name any books that could not be included on teachers' bookshelves, but Ms. Wilson made the decision to limit her own classroom library. She did this even after reading one of the books herself and deciding that it had a positive message for students considering suicide and even though she knew students could access the book in the school's library. Again, I write this without judgment of Ms. Wilson. She believed the school district would not support her if a student's parents or guardians complained, and school districts and administrators should support their teachers. Ms. Wilson's response to this wobble did restrict her stretchiness, though, and it limited which books students had access to in her classroom.

Ms. Wilson also self-censored the instruction she provided and the kinds of discussions she facilitated in class, in part because of the wobble caused from her teaching context. As discussed in Chapter 2, Ms. Wilson said she did not engage her students in deep critical study and characterized her own instruction as "nothing deep." One of the reasons she decided not to pursue CLP deeply was because, as she said, "I'm fearful of what I say."

In an interview, I asked Ms. Wilson what she believed would need to happen so she and her students could pursue critical topics in more depth and use texts as tools to critique injustice and speak back to abuses of power. She responded:

> I wish they would just leave our classrooms to us to handle. And that we would get backed up by outside sources too. Because I don't know how that will be handled at a district level if I touch on a sensitive topic.... I don't know, really just after that parent kind of lit in and the whole district kind of got into a whole uproar about [optional texts in an advanced placement course] ... I was like, "I don't want to go that route." ... I feel like the parent's always right.

In this response, Ms. Wilson referred to a situation at another high school in the district that occurred earlier in the school year. Both Mrs. Skipmann and Ms. Wilson wobbled because of this issue. They told me an Advanced Placement (AP) language and composition teacher gave students a list of optional texts to choose from to accomplish an assignment. One parent looked over the list and objected to some of the books. This parent complained about them, and their complaint made it all the way to the school board. The school board sided with the parent, and the district updated its rules for book selections as a result. It is no wonder that Ms. Wilson believed "the parent's always right." Mrs. Skipmann learned about the parent's complaint against the AP teacher through social media, and she told me that by "creeping" on social media she discovered parents and guardians in her district were organizing complaints against other ELA teachers. No wonder Ms. Wilson and Mrs. Skipmann wobbled because of the "uproar" caused by one parent.

Ms. Wilson responded to this wobble through self-censorship because she did not "want to go that route" (i.e., do something that could cause an uproar). In an interview, Ms. Wilson said, "I don't want to do anything that's going to cause a stink with a parent or make them question anything about my classroom." I doubt many teachers want to start conflicts with parents, but, as you'll see in Chapters 4, 5, 6, and 7, I encourage teachers to communicate to parents and guardians to help them appreciate what teachers are hoping to accomplish as they teach for CHANGE. I believe that teachers can help many parents and guardians see the value in CLP, or I believe that teachers, at the very least, can communicate clearly with parents and guardians to avoid causing a "stink" with them. Because Ms. Wilson doubted the support she would receive if someone did question what she did in her classroom, she responded to her wobbles by self-censoring. Her response is understandable given her teaching context, but responding to her wobbles in this way also restricted her stretchiness. She did not feel comfortable enough with wobbling to go beyond "nothing deep" in her teaching.

When Mrs. Skipmann wanted to provide CLP but knew doing so could upset parents and guardians, she wobbled. In the very first interview, she said, "It's always hanging in the back of your head, 'Am I going to get fired today?'" The fear of facing disciplinary action, especially of being terminated, caused wobble for Mrs. Skipmann, and sometimes she responded to it through self-censorship. During the first semester of observations, Mrs. Skipmann said she would not teach critical literary theories because, as she said, "discussing some of these could cause some serious parent repercussions." That semester, regarding teaching critical literary theories, her stretchiness was restricted.

At Impavid High School, Mr. Tophill too, at times, responded to wobble through self-censorship. Mr. Tophill wobbled when he considered adopting critical poses that would push him to guide his students in using texts as tools to dismantle the patriarchy (more than just understanding "what does feminism say") and to teach queer theory along with the other critical literary theories he taught. While Mr. Tophill taught feminist literary theory, he self-censored his goals for his instruction, so his stretchiness for that wobble went only so far. Additionally, Mr. Tophill did not teach queer theory, so his stretchiness for wobble was even more restricted with this theory than with feminism.

The larger forces surrounding his classroom caused Mr. Tophill to wobble regarding both critical literary theories. In an interview, Mr. Tophill said the world his students live in is both "anti-women" and "anti-queer." He added, "This stuff is embedded into them from the moment of conception, basically. And it takes so long to unlearn some of these things." Specifically regarding queer theory, Mr. Tophill's stretchiness for wobble was, in part, affected by other forces surrounding his classroom. He had been told by teachers and students at Impavid High School that his principal opposed the Genders and Sexualities Alliance club and shut it down. Additionally, the school district communicated to all teachers at the beginning of the 2022–2023 school year that they could not ask students about their pronouns. Mr. Tophill believed this policy was intended to limit or control classroom discussions related to LGBTQIA+ people and their rights. As I mentioned in the previous chapter, the state legislators where this study took place were considering a bill that would make it illegal for teachers to "advocate" for their LGBTQIA+ students. In an interview, Mr. Tophill discussed how the larger forces surrounding his teaching context impacted his willingness to teach queer theory:

> I truly think that teaching something like queer theory involves having a school district that is going to support you. Because I don't know that there's any school in America, where if you taught queer theory, there's not going to be one parent …who is [not] going to like that. And so, you're going to need that backup. I don't think I have that backup here….

Mr. Tophill had other concerns about teaching queer theory (e.g., he was worried his students would say hurtful things to their queer classmates), but his stretchiness regarding this theory was restricted, at least in part, because of the national discourse surrounding the teaching profession, especially regarding teaching about genders and sexualities.

Mrs. Skipmann was also impacted by these larger forces impacting her teaching context. Even when she did expand her stretchiness for wobble to teach critical literary theories, her stretchiness had not expanded enough for her to teach queer theory. She told me that when she contemplated teaching queer theory it scared her because many people in the school, district, and state where she worked would get angry with her for teaching it. Mrs. Skipmann responded to that wobble through self-censorship, even though, as she said, "It's something I would like to do, because I have LGBTQ students in every class…they're reading it through a queer lens already."

I hope I'm being repetitive with this point: I am not judging these teachers. Their wobbles were warranted. They had good reason to believe that some district personnel and some parents and guardians were opposed to CLP. They had good reason to believe that, if they provided CLP, they would face scrutiny and disciplinary action without the support they needed from their school district. Ms. Wilson said, "I don't know if I can sit here and have an open discussion about abortion without getting myself in trouble because I'll be on the news." As an educator, I too have responded to my wobbles through self-censorship, limiting my goals, and being careful with my words, and all these responses to my wobbles restricted my stretchiness for future ones. Without judgment, I am simply trying to use these teachers' experiences to demonstrate that the way teachers respond to wobble affects their stretchiness. Now that I have explained some of the factors that can restrict stretchiness for wobble, let's turn to the next question: What expands it?

What Expands Stretchiness?

Just as with flexibility in yoga, stretchiness expands when teachers find ways to remain committed to teaching for CHANGE as they experience wobble. Mrs. Skipmann and Mr. Tophill both found ways to keep enacting CLP. They also both pushed themselves to continue progressing in their teaching practice and in their commitment to teaching for CHANGE. They expanded their stretchiness when they responded to their wobbles by reflecting on their beliefs about teaching, finding solace in the knowledge that they were doing something they truly believed in, and reminding themselves of the integrity of their pedagogical decisions. They also expanded their stretchiness by creating rationales to support and defend their decisions. Mr. Tophill further expanded his stretchiness by enacting subversive teaching as a response to wobble.

Reflecting on Teaching Beliefs

Because Mr. Tophill taught seniors, he was determined to help them improve their writing so they could be prepared for college. When he taught critical literary theories, he required his students to read a novel of their choice and use a literary theory to write a literary analysis of their selected novel. When he experienced wobble from teaching feminism, he remained committed despite the wobble, in part because he believed it was his job to prepare students for the kinds of thinking and writing they would need to do in literature courses in college.

Mr. Tophill also believed it was important for teachers to engage in internal work so they could make pedagogical decisions that aligned with their beliefs. We discussed his dedication to teaching critical literary theories despite his wobbles at length when I returned to his classroom after the summer break. He said, "I think [the dedication is] coming from the fact that I realize it's needed. Like, I don't care if I get in trouble for something that is needed." It takes courage and conviction to risk disciplinary action, but Mr. Tophill believed he was doing what was best for his students, and this belief supported him when he experienced wobble and allowed him to expand his stretchiness. He also said, "If I'm standing in the right place, I'm good, so if stuff does hit the fan, as long as I feel like my intentions were right, and I'm standing on what students need to learn, then I'm good." Later in the same interview, Mr. Tophill said:

> It also comes with learning who you are as a person and not letting anybody falter that. Because if I know who I am as a person, you can't tell me whether I'm doing something wrong with my students. If I'm comfortable with what I'm doing, my skin, who I am as a teacher, as a human being, how can you tell me I'm wrong? And so, there's a lot of work that has to be done for people to do that.

I agree with Mr. Tophill that enacting CLP demands a lot of internal work. Mr. Tophill's beliefs demonstrate perfectly the importance of paying attention to moments of wobble because wobble signals potential for internal work and personal and professional growth: Mr. Tophill wobbled, and he responded by challenging himself to do the internal work necessary to grow.

As a final note on how Mr. Tophill's beliefs impacted his responses to wobble and therefore his stretchiness, Mr. Tophill did not believe he had done enough internal work to teach queer theory. In an interview, he reflected:

> The other thing that keeps me from doing it is I have a lot to learn about queer theory as well.... It takes so long to unlearn some of these [dominant perspectives], and even as a person standing here who has done a lot of work– who has been reflecting, I still have to unlearn a lot of things. And it's a day-to-day struggle with me, thinking, "Oh, okay, that was problematic what I just thought. I should kind of check what's going on with me."

Mr. Tophill believed that once he decided to enact CLP a certain way—if he had done the needed internal work—he was prepared to remain committed despite the wobbles he might experience. He was even willing to face disciplinary action for teaching for CHANGE. Those beliefs allowed him to enact CLP throughout the study, and in the future, they might allow him to expand his stretchiness for wobble even more. In the future, he may be able to provide instruction on queer theory.

Mrs. Skipmann's beliefs also allowed her to respond to her wobbles in ways that expanded her stretchiness. In the very first interview, she said, "At the end of the day, if they don't remember what a metaphor is but they're a better human being, then I've done my job." Mrs. Skipmann believed that her job involved more than teaching a set of standards or making students memorize definitions of literary terms. She reiterated that belief in an email later in the spring semester. She wrote:

> My students will be able to vote in 1–2 years, and I want them to be able to think critically and not just follow people/stances blindly. That belief drives me to keep having the difficult conversations, even when it's hard. I truly want to prepare all of them for life outside of [school].

Her belief that it was her job to prepare her students to be contributing citizens to society sustained Mrs. Skipmann when she experienced wobble, and when she reflected on her beliefs, she could respond to her wobble in ways that expanded her stretchiness for future ones.

Mrs. Skipmann expanded her stretchiness for wobble when she decided to teach critical literary theories like feminism and Marxism in the second semester of observations. When I asked her to reflect on the bravery she displayed in the final interview of the study, she said she decided to "to push through and do something that I feel like the kids would benefit from." Because she believed teaching those theories would help her students, she pushed through the wobble, which expanded her stretchiness.

Another belief helped her push through the wobble: Mrs. Skipmann told me that she enjoys encouraging her students to try new things to challenge themselves, like taking AP literature or AP composition and rhetoric courses. In the final interview, Mrs. Skipmann told me she decided to push herself to teach feminism and Marxism because, as she said, "I expect them to try new stuff, so why should I not expect that of myself?" Mrs. Skipmann's beliefs about the purpose of ELA instruction and the importance of personal and academic growth challenged her to enact CLP in ways she previously thought she could not handle.

Creating Rationales to Defend Teaching Decisions
When Mr. Tophill and Mrs. Skipmann decided to teach for CHANGE, they took the time to think through how they could defend their teaching decisions if someone questioned them. Mr. Tophill experienced some wobble when he decided to place more emphasis on teaching critical literary theories than on the study of British literature. When I asked him about this decision, Mr. Tophill explained it this way:

> I want my kids to be active in their learning, and it's already hard teaching British Lit. because I'm dealing with students whose first language is not English, I'm dealing with students who don't read texts outside of young adult lit… I made them read a novel. [A] 200-page novel.

> They tell me they haven't had to read a novel since middle school. So, to me, by [focusing on critical literary theories], we're still doing those standards. We're still doing the assignments. We're still looking at text evidence and things like that. We're just not doing it with British Lit. solely. And so that is how I appease myself with that decision.

When he wobbled over his decision to decenter the study of British literature in his course, he "appeased" himself by standing firm in his intentions to do what he felt was best for his students and their academic needs.

Mrs. Skipmann planned a rationale when she decided to teach critical literary theories. Before she taught them, she prepared. In an interview, she described how she got ready:

> I actually went back to some old textbooks from college and reread what I understood about it. And I did a lot of research on it.... I had a conversation with our media specialist...and I even looked up some example assignments that other people had done.... And then I made my notes based off of that.

Mrs. Skipmann believed that her students would benefit from learning these theories, so she put a lot of effort into preparing her instruction. Doing this much preparation also helped her create a rationale to defend her decision to teach them, even though she and her students knew that some parents and guardians might object. In an email, Mrs. Skipmann wrote that though feminism and Marxism have "a stigma attached that have [sic] the potential to upset a parent," she did, as she wrote, feel "confident in my ability to explain the content to a parent should they get upset, so that helped." When teaching feminism and Marxism caused Mrs. Skipmann to wobble, she reassured herself that she could defend her decisions to an upset parent or guardian, and this helped her remain committed to teaching for CHANGE.

As discussed in the previous chapter, Mrs. Skipmann, during the study, did not feel prepared to teach queer theory. When she and I discussed the wobble caused from even contemplating teaching this theory, Mrs. Skipmann said, "I'm open to it. I just think I'd want to prepare. Like, cover my butt more." If Mrs. Skipmann is able to expand her stretchiness for wobble enough to teach queer theory in the future, she will likely prepare a rationale to defend that decision.

Resisting Censorship through Subversive Teaching
Even though Mr. Tophill did not teach queer theory, he did teach one lesson in which he encouraged students to interpret a text through a queer lens—he just did not tell them that is what they were doing in the lesson. In the initial interview, as we discussed the possibility of teaching queer theory, Mr. Tophill said, "We've slowly went there but not [fully]." He told me he used a canonical British literature text—"Lanval," a poem by Marie de France—to disrupt heteronormativity and to challenge homophobia. Mr. Tophill explained, "Lanval's a knight, [and] he doesn't have sex with Queen Guinevere. And Guinevere calls him gay. And we interrogate that. And that was the way I snuck that in." This phrasing struck me; Mr. Tophill felt he had to sneak a queer lens into his instruction. Unfortunately, he taught this lesson before the study began, and I was not able to observe him teaching it the following semester, but I interpreted his use of a canonical text to interrogate homophobia and heteronormativity as an act of resistance, as subversive teaching.

Dyches et al. (2020) defined subversive teaching as "instruction that purposefully works to satisfy traditional markers of mainstream success and academic conventions (such as addressing national standards or following a prescribed curriculum) while intentionally moving students toward effecting more socially just, anti-oppressive futures" (p. 2). Mr. Tophill "snuck" a queer perspective into his teaching, even though doing so caused him to wobble. He did this by embracing subversive teaching. Mr. Tophill was able to teach this one text in this one lesson without facing disciplinary action, and his success may encourage him to continue expanding his stretchiness for future wobbles.

Why is Stretchiness Important?

Stretchiness (i.e., a teacher's current readiness or preparedness to enact CLP, even though they anticipate or will experience wobble) is important for several reasons. First, stretchiness impacts teaching decisions, so if a teacher does not have much stretchiness, they will likely self-censor their teaching and limit their goals for instruction. Second, when teachers respond to wobbles in ways that restrict their stretchiness, their students' opportunities to engage in critical literacy are limited, the status quo can remain unchallenged, and students miss out on important, meaningful class discussions and activities.

If you believe, as I do, that CLP is urgently needed in public schools across the United States (and the world), then I'm sure you see the value in expanding stretchiness. Your stretchiness for wobble will affect your students' opportunities to engage in critical literacy themselves. If you want them to Challenge injustice to Help make a difference in the world by Asking and answering tough questions and Noticing ways to Get involved and Engaged in making the world a better place, you will probably need to continue to expand your stretchiness for wobble. Finally, if you teach for CHANGE, you are going to wobble. Wobble is unavoidable, but it does not have to make your life hell. As Csikszentmihalyi (1990) explained, people can experience "the best moments in [their] lives" when they remain committed to accomplishing "something difficult and worthwhile" (p. 3). If you believe that enacting CLP is worthwhile, you can experience immense joy and happiness in your teaching career by expanding your stretchiness for wobble. Expanding your stretchiness will increase your opportunities of obtaining flow daily.

The rest of this book offers specific suggestions for providing CLP in high school ELA classrooms as well as encouragement for you to expand your stretchiness for wobble. I hope the book so far has encouraged and inspired you, and I hope the following chapters will be useful to you in your own teaching and with your personal experiences with wobble.

References

Csikszentmihalyi, M. (1990). *Flow: The psychology of optimal experience*. Harper & Row.

Diaz, J. (2022, March 28). *Florida's governor signs controversial law opponents dubbed "Don't Say Gay"*. NPR.org. https://www.npr.org/2022/03/28/1089221657/dontsay-gay-florida-desantis

Dobie, A. B. (2009). *Theory into practice: An introduction to literary criticism* (2nd ed.). Wadsworth Cengage Learning.

Dyches, J., Sams, B., & Boyd, A. S. (Eds.). (2020). *Acts of resistance: Subversive teaching in the English language arts classroom*. Myers Education Press.

Fecho, B. (2011). *Teaching for the students: Habits of heart, mind, and practice in the engaged classroom*. Teachers College Press.

Fecho, B., Graham, P., & Hudson-Ross, S. (2005). Appreciating the wobble: Teacher research, professional development, and figured worlds. *English Education, 37*(3), 174–199.

Garcia, A., & O'Donnell-Allen, C. (2015). *Pose, wobble, flow: A culturally proactive approach to literacy instruction*. Teachers College Press.

4

What Could Critical Literacy Pedagogy Look Like in Grade 9?

Critical scholars and literacy researchers agree: High school students need their teachers to help them gain access to the literacies valued in the fields related to English language arts (ELA) (see Janks, 2000; Moje, 2015; Morrell 2008). Students need to learn, for example, how to read, puzzle over, and arrive at their own interpretation of a piece of fiction (Rainey, 2017). I use *valued literacies* and *dominant literacies* as synonyms to mean the things that people in the fields related to ELA (e.g., like journalism, literary criticism, college English, rhetoric, composition, creative writing, and technical writing) value and do with texts. From a critical perspective, what is valued in the fields related to ELA is about power. Those with the power to influence institutions of learning have helped decide what literacies are embraced in ELA (like analyzing a poem, and really, there are specific ways to do that depending on the poem and the literary theory influencing a person's interpretation) and which ones are not. To be able to participate fully in the fields related to ELA outside of school, students need access to the dominant literacies of those fields.

Access by itself, though, is not enough. Educators must ask, access for what purpose? Teachers providing critical literacy pedagogy (CLP) want to help their students gain access to the dominant literacies so they can use them to reimagine and rewrite the world they live in as they speak to, speak back to, and speak against power and injustice. Teachers providing CLP want their students to have access to valued literacies so they can use those literacies for CHANGE.

As professor Elizabeth Moje (2008) argued, students need access to the valued ways that knowledge is produced and communicated in ELA so that what counts as knowledge and what counts as valued communication "can be routinely or more explicitly challenged and reshaped," so students can become "critical readers and thinkers" (pp. 102–103). Students should learn how to write literary analysis, argumentative and expository essays, and they should learn how to compose them well, using craft and style to make their points and demonstrate creative thinking and original insights (i.e., access), but they should also be encouraged to use their access to these dominant literacies as ways of challenging the status quo and speaking to (and speaking back to) power.

ELA in grade 9 in the U.S. often introduces students to different literary genres and how to interpret and analyze them. Most grade 9 ELA curricula include informational texts and some argumentative and expository writing. Because this is their first ELA class in high school, grade 9 ELA classrooms are perfect places to help students continue to gain access to the dominant literacies. The setting is also ideal for encouraging them to use their access to redesign what counts as knowledge, which literacies are valued, whose literacies are valued, and what texts should be studied and produced. Grade 9 ELA classrooms are great places to teach for CHANGE.

One crucial question that ELA teachers hoping to implement CLP must ask is what is the purpose of ELA instruction? If it is simply to make students memorize the symbols in a short story or to state the theme of a play, perhaps ELA instruction helps students gain access to the valued literacies. (More than likely, such instruction simply requires students to memorize what the teacher said in class or plagiarize from the internet.) If teachers believe the purpose of ELA instruction is to help students gain access to dominant literacies so they can use those literacies as a way of making the world more just and equitable, they will teach for CHANGE, which will support our students in making tangible differences in the world.

Opportunities for Critical Literacy Pedagogy with Grade 9 Curriculum

In general, the opportunities for CLP with grade 9 curricula will be the same for the other grades in high school (see Chapter 1), but the traditional grade 9 curriculum offers unique possibilities to engage students in speaking to, speaking back to, and speaking against power and injustice. Texts like *The Odyssey* by Homer and *Romeo and Juliet* by Shakespeare are often studied in grade 9. Students also read several poems and short stories. As they study these texts, students begin to gain access to the knowledge and literacies valued in ELA. The texts that students typically study (and the valued knowledge they are expected to learn from studying these texts) are full of possibilities for CLP.

The epic poem *The Odyssey* presents exciting opportunities for students to participate in critical literacy. For example, teachers can design lessons to engage students in disrupting some harmful messages a noncritical reading of the epic could communicate, like toxic masculinity. *Toxic* masculinity, as opposed to healthy masculinity, celebrates violence and villainizes women's sexuality (Steiss, 2020). Jacob Steiss described the CLP he provided to his ninth graders in an all-boys private school. As they studied *The Odyssey*, Steiss created classroom activities designed to counter toxic masculinity: Steiss guided students in critically analyzing the epic with questions like "What voices are privileged, and which are left out?", "What stereotypes are perpetuated?", and "How can we redress these problems? How can we use this analysis to create more justice or equity?" (p. 436). Steiss also had his students rewrite scenes from the epic from the perspectives of marginalized characters. Reflecting on the unit, Steiss felt that disrupting canonical texts "can allow students to speak out against important social issues" (p. 439). You may want to borrow some of these activities from Steiss if you teach *The Odyssey*.

Good teaching connects what students study to their everyday literacies, lives, cultures, and what matters to them. CLP seeks to make what students study relevant to their lives too, but it wants to make those connections to support students in taking action to make the world better. Educators McNary and Rodríguez (2020) suggest connecting *The Odyssey* to social justice issues surrounding U.S. immigration policies and laws. For many students, issues of immigration are of the utmost importance for them, their friends, and their families. In McNary and Rodríguez's teaching, they have used *The Odyssey*, along with suggestions from "Epic Explorations: Teaching the 'Odyssey' with *The New York Times*" by Goble and Wiersum (2019), to engage students in investigating U.S. immigration policy under the administration of Donald Trump. Their students considered questions like "by whom is *foreign* or *foreigner* (migrant, emigrant, immigrant) used, and for what purposes—then and today?" (p. 202). Using the epic as a way of thinking about questions surrounding immigration today connected a canonical text to students' lives and concerns. Creating activities that result in students asking such tough questions supports them in realizing that the way the world is now is not the way it must be—a better, more just world is possible. Such activities help students see they can be part of making needed CHANGE.

Shakespeare's *Romeo and Juliet* (R&J) is another canonical text often studied in grade 9 that teachers can use for critique and resistance (see the suggested R&J Issues Unit below). Teachers can use the play as a tool to engage students in asking and answering tough questions about gang violence and researching productive ways that communities and local, state, and federal governments can address gang violence. Studying the play does not have to stop at teaching students the drama terms they need to know or the plot of the play. This play features several topics relevant to students' lives (e.g., violence, sex, hiding things from parents/guardians, and teen suicide), and teachers can use the text as a tool to get students doing things in class (and maybe outside of class) to envision a better world and perhaps produce texts and projects that advocate for the world they've envisioned. Below, I describe a unit you can use while teaching *Romeo and Juliet* that Challenges injustice to Help make a difference by Asking and answering tough questions and Noticing ways to Get involved and Engaged in making the world better.

Overview of the R&J Issues Unit for CHANGE

Before I share the specifics of this suggested Unit for CHANGE, I explain a few things and provide an overview of the unit. First, though *Romeo and Juliet* is part of a literary canon that has often been used to marginalize students, it has lots of potential to empower students to consider issues of justice that matter to them. Many parents and guardians expect their children to study this play in high school, but I'm encouraging teachers to teach it differently than the way it has been traditionally taught, as an act of subversion (see Dyches et al., 2020). I'm encouraging teachers to use this canonical text as a tool to challenge issues of power to promote social justice and as a way for students to speak back to and speak against abuses of power.

The R&J Issues Unit is meant to be implemented during the study of the play. If you decide you might want to try this unit, just remember I've written it assuming that all the things traditionally taught about the play, like dramatic irony, plot, characterization, and theme, will be covered. I'm suggesting this unit as part of a thorough study of the play. Students do need access, after all, to the knowledge and literacies valued in ELA. The lesson plan ideas I offer below are for the lessons specifically designed to engage students in critical literacy as they study the play.

The R&J Issues Unit for Change engages students in two main enterprises: First, they will ask and answer tough questions about the issues that Shakespeare seems to deal with so flippantly, like the issue of sexual consent and the issue of teenage suicide. Second, they will continue asking and answering tough questions by investigating why Shakespeare's play featuring teenage sex is celebrated (and often required reading) but other texts for young adults featuring sex are being challenged and banned.

As an overview, the unit engages students in considering several important questions and topics. They will consider that in some U.S. states, if *Romeo and Juliet* took place today, Romeo could be arrested and labeled a sex offender because Juliet is only 13 (Beck & Boys, 2012). Students will learn about the record book-banning efforts in school and public libraries (Harris & Alter, 2023). Considering the content they are often required to read when they study *Romeo and Juliet* (i.e., violence, teenage sex, and suicide), the unit will encourage students to challenge, or at least to question, book bans. For example, Ashley Hope Pérez's book *Out of Darkness* was challenged by a parent who disliked some of the sexual descriptions in the novel, and Pérez questioned why teenage sex is "fine in Shakespeare" but not in her book (as cited in McLaughlin, 2022, para 8). Students' main assignment is to write an argumentative essay addressing concerns about which texts are appropriate for high schoolers to study in class or have access to in school and classroom libraries. They will be required to evaluate the appropriateness of Shakespeare's play compared to a young adult (YA) novel they choose to read during the unit. Based on their evaluation of both texts, they should argue if both, only one, or neither is appropriate for ninth graders to study in school. They will cite evidence from both *Romeo and Juliet* and the book they selected to support their points.

At the start of the unit, students will select a challenged YA book to read (see my suggested list of books below) individually as they study the play as a class. While I recommend that students write an argumentative essay at the conclusion of the unit, you could adjust this to be multimodal or require some sort of performance or oral presentation. Your students could create a video essay or write a book review and post it online. Whatever form their evaluative thinking takes, that's the point of this unit: Their task is to think critically and to evaluate the challenged book they selected to address whether they think it is or is not appropriate for teens.

If I were to teach this unit, I would hope students could Challenge injustice to Help make a difference by Answering tough questions and Noticing ways to Get involved and Engaged by supporting their school and local public libraries. You could help your students speak out against book bans at School Board or Library Board meetings. Your students could write letters to district superintendents or people in congress to advocate for teens to have access to texts written by diverse authors, even if these texts occasionally feature sex scenes or discuss teen suicide. You and your students could create and record book talks about the challenged books they selected to be shared on the school library's social media account. You could collaborate with your school librarian to do a book display and have your students' book talks play on a television or monitor in the library. Your students could present their arguments to other English classes at your school. It is also possible your students could do something beyond the walls of school by working as a class to raise money to donate to The Jason Foundation, Inc. or The Trevor Project Organization, which both focus on addressing teen suicide and supporting youth. Of course, these are just some ideas, and I'm hoping you and your students will enjoy thinking of additional ways to advocate for CHANGE.

Suggested Challenged Books
- *Me and Earl and the Dying Girl* by Jesse Andrews
- *Flamer* by Mike Curato
- *We Deserve Monuments* by Jas Hammonds
- *Out of Darkness* by Ashley Hope Pérez
- *Eleanor & Park* by Rainbow Rowell
- *Forgive Me, Leonard Peacock* by Matthew Quick

The R&J Issues Unit Lesson Plans

Remember you will want to have students read the YA novels they selected during the study of the play. If your curriculum schedule allows, you may want to devote class time to literature circles (Daniels, 1994) so students can discuss their novels in groups. I suggest you have students make their novel selections after you teach the R&J Issues Unit first lesson plan.

R&J Issues Unit Lesson Plan 1

When to implement this lesson:	After you've introduced students to the play but before they've started reading it
Lesson objective:	Students will analyze claims in favor of book bans and claims against book bans to understand the current controversy regarding the appropriateness of certain texts for teens.
Assessment:	Students will complete an "Exit Ticket" asking them to list the most convincing claim for and against book bans they read about in today's lesson.

(Continued)

Suggested text needed:	"Banned Books: Top 3 Pros and Cons" by ProCon.org (2024). The link is in the references at the end of the chapter.
Suggested activities:	♦ Begin with an anticipation guide with statements about book bans and hand the guide to each student. Students will individually decide if they agree or disagree with the statements you've included. An example statement could be "No book should ever be banned from school and public libraries." Another statement could be "Books with sex scenes should never be studied for school." The statements should not be ambiguous, and students should decide if they agree or disagree with each one. ♦ After students have completed their anticipation guide, display each anticipation guide statement individually and invite students to state if they agreed or disagreed with the statement and to explain their choice. Allow students to discuss. ♦ Next, have students read and take some notes on "Banned Books: Top 3 Pros and Cons." ♦ Then engage students in a collaborative discussion activity about what they have just read. Label one side of the room "Pro" and the other side "Con," leaving the middle of the room for those who are undecided. Display, one at a time, the top 3 pros and cons. Students should move to the wall (or stay seated if they are undecided) that matches their view. Ask students to share the most compelling reason they just read about that influenced their choice. ♦ Describe the argumentative essay assignment for this unit to students. ♦ Have students complete the "Exit Ticket" for the day to wrap up the lesson.

R&J Issues Unit Lesson Plan 2

When to implement this lesson:	After students have studied Act I
Lesson objective:	Students will perform a close read of Act I, scene 1 to gather evidence so they can participate in a class discussion addressing this question: "Is this content appropriate to be studied in school?"

(Continued)

Assessment:	Students will record notes on their close reading of the scene, and they will record notes during a group discussion.
Suggested text needed:	A copy of the play (I use The Arden Shakespeare version of *Romeo and Juliet* [Shakespeare, 2012], edited by René Weis)

Suggested activities:	♦ Tell students they will work with a partner to reread Act I, scene 1. Their purpose is to determine if it is appropriate for them to study in school.
	♦ Give students a teacher-made handout with guiding questions you want them to answer. I suggest the following instructions/questions:
	  ○ Read lines 1–17 to answer these questions: Shakespeare scholars believe he uses wordplay with the words *move, stir*, and *stand* to suggest sexual arousal. How does that interpretation change the meaning of these lines, particularly Samson's? What do you think Samson means when he says he will "thrust" Montague's "maids to the wall"? (*Maid* in Shakespeare's day implied the person was a virgin.)
	  ○ Read lines 20–31 to answer these questions: Pay attention to the pun about cutting off the maids' heads. *Maidenhead* can mean a person's virginity. What do you think Samson really means he plans to do with the women he's discussing? What act is associated with violence in these lines?
	  ○ Read lines 29–35 to answer these questions: What innuendos do you think are present in these lines? Are these appropriate for school?
	  ○ As a final question, I suggest that the pairs of students answer the overarching question of the lesson: Is this scene appropriate for us to study in school? Why/why not?
	♦ Finally, ask the pairs of students to get into groups of four to evaluate the scene and determine if it was appropriate for them to have studied in class. Require students to cite the play, regardless of their evaluation. If time allows, encourage each group to share their evaluation with the class.

R&J Issues Unit Lesson Plan 3

When to implement this lesson:	After students have studied Acts I–III
Lesson objectives:	Students will determine the central idea of an opinion piece, citing evidence as support, and they will write a summary of the text.
Assessment:	Students will write a summary of the article and a statement identifying the author's main point and supporting evidence.
Suggested text needed:	"Parents Shouldn't Let Schools Force Kids to Read Smut," opinion piece by Jenni White (2016), published by *The Federalist* online magazine (the link is in the references at the end of the chapter)

Suggested activities:	♦ As you introduce students to the opinion piece, explain to them the purpose for reading the text: They are reading it to continue to consider what is appropriate for students to read in school.
	♦ Then have students work with a partner to read and summarize the piece. You will want to print this out so students can annotate it as they read. I suggest you label the paragraphs with a number to make it easier for students to reference evidence from the text. Specifically, students should work with their partner to accomplish the following tasks:
	   ◦ First, they should read the paragraphs under each bold heading (stopping once they've finished reading a section to annotate it before moving on to the next section).
	   ◦ Annotate the text by highlighting the sentences they think show the main point of each section or that they think state the author's claims and by circling key evidence the author used to support their points.
	   ◦ Then they should discuss each section and write a summary in the margins.
	♦ Repeat the tasks above until they've annotated and summarized the whole piece.
	♦ Finally, in two or three sentences, they should write an answer to this question: What were the author's main point and key pieces of evidence?
	♦ As time allows, have sets of partners form groups of four to share their summaries with each other.

R&J Issues Unit Lesson Plan 4

When to implement this lesson:	Immediately after Lesson Plan 3
Lesson objective:	Students will analyze and evaluate White's opinion piece by examining their use of rhetoric and evaluating the effectiveness of the argument.
Assessment:	Students will reread the opinion piece to analyze and evaluate how the author made and supported their points. Students will record examples of the author's use of rhetorical devices, counterclaims, and evidence, and they will use these notes to participate in a class discussion evaluating the opinion piece.
Suggested text needed:	Jenni White's opinion piece "Parents Shouldn't Let Schools Force Kids to Read Smut"
Suggested activities:	♦ Provide instruction on some rhetorical devices like appeals to logic, emotion, or values (i.e., ethics) as well as examples of claims and counterclaims. ♦ Give students a handout to complete to help them take notes on the author's use of these devices. I suggest you create a chart where the left-hand column has spaces for students to write down a paragraph number, the next column has space for students to write a shortened version of the text, another column has space for students to write what rhetorical device they think this is an example of, and a final column for them to write if they think the author was successful and explain their reasoning. ♦ Before you engage students in a collaborative rereading of the opinion piece, tell them that *The Federalist* is a politically conservative online magazine and that part of evaluating a piece is being aware of potential bias. As you read the opinion piece, stop and discuss with the class any examples of the author's use of rhetorical devices they think they noticed. You should be prepared to point out some to model for students how to complete the chart you created for them. ♦ Once you've reread the piece and students have completed their chart, ask them to prepare for a class discussion on the effectiveness of this piece.

(Continued)

	◆ Have the class discussion the next day. I'm sure you know how to conduct class discussions, but I always suggest starting a class discussion with a reminder of classroom rules and norms. I also print out example sentence starters and tape them to each student's desk so they can practice using the discourse valued in respectful discussions. For example, I might use some sentence starters they can use to participate in scholarly discourse. To help students state their opinion and defend it with evidence, they could use this sentence starter: "The author suggests [blank.] Notice what they wrote on page [blank]." To help students disagree respectfully, they could use this sentence starter: "That is one perspective, but I have a different one. What if we view it this way: [blank]?" To keep the discussion going, students could use this sentence starter: "What other perspectives are there, or who has something to say but has not been able to yet?" ◆ If time allows, once the discussion is over, have students reflect on their participation by answering questions like "How did I contribute to the class discussion? Did I contribute mostly by being a good listener, or did I contribute verbally or virtually to the discussion?" and "What would I do differently the next time we have a discussion?"

R&J Issues Unit Lesson Plan 5[1]

When to implement this lesson:	After students have studied Act III
Lesson objective:	Students will closely reread Act III, scene 2 in which Juliet expresses her desire to have sex with Romeo and an informational text about sexual consent to consider issues of sexual consent.
Assessment:	Preparation for and participation in the class discussion
Suggested texts needed:	◆ A copy of the play ◆ A teacher-made handout with facts about sexual consent, specifically for youth. I suggest the following content for the handout based on the Society for Adolescent Health and Medicine's (2023) position paper which promotes sexual consent principles in the health care of youth (this source is in the refences, and you can follow the DOI to get a PDF copy of the entire report):

(Continued)

	○ "The 2021 Youth Risk Behavior Survey of high school students in the United States (US) demonstrated that approximately 14% of females and 4% of males have experienced nonconsensual sexual activity" (p. 205). ○ "Sexual consent is one's voluntary, sober, and conscious willingness to engage in a particular sexual activity including kissing, hugging, touching, manual penetration, and sexual intercourse (oral, vaginal, or anal) with a particular person within a particular context" (p. 206). ○ "All individuals must agree to any sexual activity—every single time—for it to be consensual" (p. 206).

Suggested activities:	♦ Before having students close-read the scene, remind them of book-banning efforts; this will help them understand the purpose of close-reading Act III, scene 2: to determine if it is appropriate for them to study the scene in school.
	♦ Place students with a partner to close-read the scene.
	♦ Give students a teacher-made handout with guiding questions you want them to work with their partner to answer. I suggest the following instructions/questions:
	  ○ Read lines 1–31 to answer these questions: Why does Juliet say "gallop apace"? What does "love-performing night" mean? What is Juliet waiting for eagerly and impatiently?
	  ○ Reread lines 10–20 to answer these questions: *Maidenhead* can mean a person's virginity. Keeping in mind what Juliet is eagerly waiting for, what do you think she means by "lose a winning match"? This is an oxymoron, so what could Juliet lose while still winning?
	  ○ As a final question, I suggest the pairs of students answer the overarching question of the lesson: Keeping in mind that Juliet is 13, is this scene appropriate for us to study in school? Why/why not?
	♦ Then have students read and take notes on the handout about sexual consent.
	♦ After students have had time to read the scene closely and apply what they learned from the handout, engage them in a class discussion about sexual consent and if Juliet indeed can consent to sex with Romeo.

R&J Issues Unit Lesson Plan 6

When to implement this lesson:	As students are reading Act IV
Lesson objectives:	Students will determine the central idea of an opinion piece, citing evidence as support, and they will write a summary of the text.
Assessment:	Students will write a summary of the article and a statement identifying the author's main point and supporting evidence.
Suggested text needed:	"The School Library Used to be a Sanctuary," opinion piece by Martha Hickson (2022), published by CNN (the link is in the references at the end of the chapter)
Suggested activities:	Because students will likely benefit from doing the same activities with different texts, the suggested activities for this lesson are the same as those for Lesson Plan 3, so please review that lesson for the specific suggestions: ♦ As you introduce students to the opinion piece, explain to them the purpose for reading the text: to continue to consider what is appropriate for students to read in school. Encourage them to make connections between the content of *Romeo and Juliet* and Hickson's main argument in this piece. ♦ Have students work with a partner to read and summarize the piece. This piece does not have section headings, so when you print copies for students, I suggest you "chunk" the text for them so they can read, annotate, and summarize sections of the piece. Specifically, students should work with their partner to accomplish the same tasks as in Lesson Plan 3. ♦ As time allows, have sets of partners form groups of four to share their summaries with each other.

R&J Issues Unit Lesson Plan 7

When to implement this lesson:	Immediately after Lesson Plan 6
Lesson objective:	Students will analyze and evaluate Hickson's opinion piece by examining their use of rhetoric and evaluating the effectiveness of the argument.

(Continued)

Assessment:	Students will reread the opinion piece to analyze and evaluate how the author made and supported their points. Students will record examples of the author's use of rhetorical devices, counterclaims, and evidence, and they will use these notes to participate in a class discussion evaluating the opinion piece.
Suggested text needed:	Hickson's opinion piece "The School Library Used to be a Sanctuary"
Suggested activities:	Again, I believe students will benefit from repeating the same activities with different texts, so the suggested activities for this lesson are mostly the same as they were for Lesson Plan 4: ♦ Give students a handout to complete to help them take notes on the author's use of these devices. I suggest you use the same chart you created for Lesson Plan 4. ♦ Before you engage students in a collaborative rereading of the opinion piece, tell them this article is linked in a report produced by the American Library Association arguing against book bans. Remind them that a crucial aspect of evaluating a piece is being aware of potential bias. As you read the opinion piece, stop and discuss with the class any examples of the author's use of rhetorical devices they think they noticed. ♦ Once you've reread the piece and students have completed their chart, ask them to prepare for a class discussion the next day on the effectiveness of this piece. ♦ Have the class discussion the next day. Please see Lesson Plan 4 and review my suggestions for facilitating class discussions.

R&J Issues Unit Lesson Plan 8[2]

When to implement this lesson:	After students have finished reading and analyzing the play
Lesson objective:	Students will closely read Act V, scene 3 to gather evidence so they can participate in a class discussion addressing this question: "What messages are we receiving about violence, sex, love, and suicide by studying this play?"

(Continued)

Assessment:	Students will record notes on their close reading of the scene, record notes during the discussion, and reflect on their participation in the discussion.
Suggested text needed:	A copy of the play
Suggested activities:	♦ Place students with a partner to close-read Act V, scene 3. ♦ Give students a teacher-made handout with guiding questions you want them to work with their partner to answer. I suggest the following instructions/questions: 　○ Read lines 90–96 and 101–110 to answer these questions: What about Juliet does Romeo seemed focused on even as he believes she is dead? What message do you think that sends about love? 　○ Read lines 106–121 to answer these questions: How quickly does it seem that Romeo decides to die by suicide? What message do these lines send readers about love and death? 　○ Read lines 160–171 to answer these questions: When Juliet hopes there is still potent poison on Romeo's lips, she calls it a "friendly drop." What does this wording indicate about Juliet's views of her own death? What message do you think her eagerness for death sends to young teens about romance, love, and suicide? Do you think these messages are harmful? Explain. Some have interpreted Juliet's suicide by Romeo's dagger to be a sexually suggestive metaphor. Considering the sexual innuendoes in Act I comparing sexual organs to weapons, do you think this is a fair interpretation? Explain. 　○ As a final question, I suggest the pairs of students answer the overarching question of the lesson: What messages are we receiving about violence, sex, love, and suicide by studying this play? ♦ Once partners have had time to read these lines closely and consider the messages, engage students in a class discussion for the rest of the lesson.

R&J Issues Unit Lesson Plan 9

When to implement this lesson:	After students have finished reading and analyzing the play and their selected novels
Lesson objective:	Students will prepare for and participate in a class discussion evaluating the appropriateness of studying *Romeo and Juliet* in school.
Assessment:	Students will record notes to prepare for the discussion, record notes during the discussion, and reflect on their participation in the discussion.
Suggested texts needed:	Copies of the play and students' self-selected YA novels
Suggested activities:	♦ Begin by reminding students of their argumentative essay assignment that requires them to evaluate Shakespeare's play and the novel they have read. Tell them to take notes during the discussion to prepare to write their essay. ♦ Review, as you see fit, some of the points that students have already made, and the evidence that they provided, in previous class discussions. ♦ Engage the students in a discussion on the appropriateness of studying Shakespeare's play in school.

R&J Issues Unit Lesson Plan 10

When to implement this lesson:	Immediately after Lesson Plan 9
Lesson objectives:	Students will compare the content of Shakespeare's play to the content in the YA novel they read. Students will judge the appropriateness of the two texts and gather and document evidence to support their comparison and evaluation of the texts.
Assessment:	Students will use a Venn Diagram graphic organizer to support their analysis and evaluation of the texts.
Suggested texts needed:	Copies of the play, students' self-selected YA novels, and the opinion pieces students have studied

(Continued)

Suggested activities:	♦ Revisit students' responses to the Anticipation Guide statements they responded to in Lesson Plan 1. Allow for a quick class discussion and ask students to consider if any of their opinions has changed since the start of the unit. ♦ Give students a copy of a Venn Diagram graphic organizer which will require them to consider the similarities and differences between the content of the play and their selected YA novels. Students should consider things like the potential "controversial" topics covered in each text, how they were described, the authors' treatment of the topics, and if the topics were handled appropriately for students in grade 9. ♦ Model how to complete the Venn Diagram and then allow students to work independently. ♦ By the end of class, require students to write a statement declaring their judgment: Are the texts appropriate for ninth graders? Why/why not?

Anticipated Moments of Wobble with the R&J Issues Unit

If you're thinking that doing this unit would cause too much wobble (i.e., tension, dread, and doubt) for you to handle, I understand. I wobbled as I created it. I wobbled when suggesting challenged books to use for this unit. *Flamer* by Mike Curato addresses adolescent sexuality and suicidal ideation. Those are topics that can quickly get parents/guardians, administrators, and even students upset, but they are important for young people to think through, especially in nonjudgmental environments with support from their peers and teachers. I also wobbled because *Me and Earl and the Dying Girl* by Jesse Andrews is challenged because of its descriptions of sexual acts. Yes, we all know Romeo and Juliet have sex in the play, but Shakespeare does not actually describe the sex. I don't want to sound like a prude, but I also don't want to give the impression that if you're nervous about encouraging youth to read books with sex scenes in them there's something wrong with you. Each person experiences wobble uniquely, and if you're experiencing wobble because of these suggested YA novels, that's okay!

I want to be clear: I don't advocate that you *force* your students to read a specific challenged book. And I've been careful to use the word *challenged* instead of *banned*. I'm terribly sorry if a book is banned in your school, district, or state. I hate the idea that people are banning books written for teens, especially because most of the books being banned are by people of color or members of LGBTQIA+ communities (Harris & Alter, 2023). I hate it, but I don't want to encourage anyone to do something that will get them fired or in legal trouble. I'm suggesting that you give your students choices of books to read, from a list of books that have been challenged, to help them investigate what topics adults feel are acceptable for them to read.

Anticipated Moments of Wobble with Specific Lesson Plans

The first lesson plan introduces students to the topic of banned books. Because the ProCon.org reading presents points from two different perspectives, I do not anticipate that this would create much wobble for you. If it does, please remember that this lesson helps students form their own informed opinions by showing them facts and opinions on this national debate that impacts what texts teens have access to in schools.

The second lesson plan, though, might cause some wobble because it intentionally draws students' attention to the sexual innuendo used early in the play. Again, I don't want to come across as a prude, but it might be a little uncomfortable to require students to read closely a scene that makes dick jokes. Please remember that you didn't write the innuendos; you're just helping your students read a text closely. Second, you are helping your students think evaluatively and critically.

The third and fourth lesson plans require students to read and evaluate a text that would likely cause some wobble. The opinion piece cites graphic scenes from challenged books to make the point that schools should not require students to read "smut." The author quotes passages that use the word *fuck*, for example. This article was written not for high school students but for their parents or guardians. I suggest you copy the text and create an ad-free version with word-processing software that you can print. As you do that, I suggest you use ellipses to replace the graphic scenes the author quotes (the quoted scenes are not from required reading for grade 9 students). And I suggest you include PG descriptions of the quotes the author presented so students can still evaluate the evidence without reading a description of sexual violence. I think this would allow them to engage in closely reading a relevant, informational text but would protect you from accusations that you made students read graphic sex scenes in class. While this text may cause you some wobble, remember it is published by a conservative online magazine, so if someone accuses you of indoctrinating or imposing an agenda on students, you can show them that you've assigned a text emphasizing a politically conversative perspective on the issue.

The fifth lesson plan, like the second, might cause some wobble because it engages students in another close reading of a scene that addresses the issue of sexual consent. Just like with Lesson Plan 2, though, these issues are in the play, and as I've written in my example letter to parents and guardians (see Appendix B), this is an important issue that teens need to discuss so they can be safe in school. Sadly, teens experience sexual assault, so why not take this opportunity to address it responsibly?

Because the opinion piece that students will read in Lesson Plan 6 and evaluate in Lesson Plan 7 is against book-banning efforts and clearly criticizes some of the completely inappropriate behavior of parents, guardians, and community members who are attempting to ban books, assigning this text might cause some wobble. You may feel like you are making your personal views too obvious to students, which always brings with it the possibility that you will be accused of indoctrinating them. If you feel this way, just remember the other opinion piece students read in Lesson Plan 3. Presenting two biased texts offering two different opinions to your students helps them think for themselves.

Just like Lesson Plans 2 and 5, the eighth lesson has students close-reading the play to consider seriously the issue of teenage suicide. First, I want to emphasize the importance of collaborating with school counselors and having resources available to students. Doing so shows them, your administrators, and students' parents and guardians that you care about your students' well-being. Second, remember, Shakespeare brought these topics up, not you. This lesson addresses this topic in a healthy way, giving it the gravity it deserves.

The class discussion in Lesson Plan 9 might cause some wobble for you because you might be nervous that some students may make inappropriate statements. Let's be real, though: When is that not a potential risk? Students say inappropriate things all day long at school, so this is not a new threat. If you are experiencing a lot of wobble about this, I suggest that you and your students spend some more time discussing and understanding your classroom norms and what it means to respect someone's opinion.

Encouragement to Expand Your Stretchiness

If you like the idea of the R&J Issues Unit for Change but feel some discomfort or unease (i.e., some wobble), that's totally understandable. I'd like to encourage you, though, to expand your stretchiness. My suggestions are that you (1) collaborate with your English teacher peers, school administrators, and parents/guardians; (2) adjust the unit as you see fit for your classroom; (3) create a rationale you can use to defend your pedagogical decisions if needed; and (4) spend some time reflecting on where your discomfort is coming from and what that can tell you about your teaching practice and your needs as a human and teacher.

Collaborate with Your English Teacher Peers, School Administrators, and Parents/Guardians

If you work in a school that encourages and supports collaboration amongst teachers, please take advantage of that! If you're thinking about trying out the R&J Issues Unit, share this unit with your peers who will be teaching the play too. Together, you can tailor my lesson plan suggestions to better fit your school. Together, you can also revise my suggested letter to parents and guardians (see Appendix B). It is much easier to experience wobble when you're working with someone who supports you and is going through something similar. During my dissertation research, Mr. Tophill specifically stated that he wished he could work with other ELA teachers when designing units because he desired that support and acknowledgement that providing CLP is challenging work. You may have to be the one to get the conversation going, but teaching this unit will likely go much more smoothly for you if you've collaborated with your peers. Also, it will likely be much easier to get the needed backing and support from your administrators if three or four teachers will be doing the same unit.

Making sure your school administrators understand the value of the R&J Issues Unit before you implement it could really save you a lot of grief. I've brainstormed some points you could use as a rationale (included below) that you could present to your administration. If you've collaborated with other grade 9 ELA teachers, you could ask the administrators to meet with you all so you could explain the unit to them before you implement it. You could listen to and address their concerns. Such a meeting would give them a chance to prepare to support you in the case of a complaint. Additionally, you could prepare a list of things you'd like to ask the administrators to do to support your efforts.

I want to be careful not to present parents and guardians as opponents. Yes, the number one thing the teachers in my dissertation research were afraid of was the possibility of upsetting parents and guardians who would complain and get the teachers in trouble. I respect their concern and fear. Still, parents and guardians want to be involved in their teens' education. They want to help their teens if they're experiencing suicidal ideation, and they want to make sure their teens stay safe regarding sexual activity. I suggest letting them know about the unit, what books are on the list of challenged books you plan to let students use to select their book, why those books are on the list, and the purpose of the unit (see my example letter to parents and guardians in Appendix B). This unit is meant to empower students to speak to, speak back to, and speak against power and injustice to effect needed CHANGE. Many parents/guardians would support that, and they are key stakeholders who could help you accomplish your goals.

Adjust the Unit

As you remember, Garcia and O'Donnell-Allen (2015) compared experiencing and responding to wobble to practicing yoga. When a yoga practitioner decides to try a pose, they may wobble. They may find that their limbs are not limber enough or that their standing foot is struggling to balance their weight. To continue practicing the pose, then, the yoga practitioner must respond in some way to the messages their body is giving them. When I practice yoga, for example, I adjust where I'm reaching because I'm not flexible. Adjusting allows me to continue practicing the pose, even though my body isn't stretchy enough to imitate the yoga instructor. You can make needed adjustments to the R&J Issues Unit too.

Instead of having students read the challenged books, for example, you could have students read the opinion pieces about book bans that I included in the lesson plans. They could read just the articles—that way, they're not reading the sex scenes that may have caused you to wobble. You could still have students read the scenes from the play I highlighted in the Lesson Plans above and have students evaluate *Romeo and Juliet* to determine if they think it was appropriate for them to read or not. Students could then write an argumentative essay addressing the appropriateness of *Romeo and Juliet* considering recent book-banning efforts. This approach to the R&J Issues Unit could help you avoid accusations that you intentionally made students read salacious texts, but it would still allow you to teach for CHANGE. Students could nevertheless speak at a Library Board or School Board meeting to push back against book-banning efforts. Adjusting the unit in this way would allow you to implement the suggested lesson plans, for the most part. If you try out the unit in this way, you could support your students in practicing critical literacy, but you would probably also spare yourself wobbles that you don't think you're prepared to handle quite yet. I encourage you to try it out with small adjustments, and in doing so, you might expand your stretchiness to the point where, someday soon, you could do the R&J Issues Unit as I initially described it or, better yet, your own version that's better than mine!

Create a Rationale

If you decide to do the R&J Issues Unit (even with slight adjustments), you will likely benefit from preparing a rationale to defend your pedagogical decisions. This is something Mrs. Skipmann and Mr. Tophill did when they experienced wobble. When Mrs. Skipmann anticipated wobble because of texts she planned to have her students study or class discussions she planned to facilitate, she created a rationale "to cover [her] butt," as she said. As you prepare your rationale, think about your teaching philosophy and what you feel is most important in ELA instruction. That will help you defend your teaching decisions. Of course, you'd want to think through this fully for yourself, but here are some points I think could help you justify teaching the R&J Issues Unit:

♦ The play, which is often required reading, contains teen sex and suicide, but the play does not address these serious topics in a way that could help your students or in a way that appreciates the issues associated with these topics. Doing this unit encourages students to think about the topics they encounter in *Romeo and Juliet* and what they can learn about them that matters in their lives. For example, students might read a challenged book that addresses sexual consent. Shakespeare doesn't mention consent. But consent is crucial for young people to understand and apply to their lives. Also, Romeo and Juliet die by suicide, but the text of the play offers no support for students who have suicidal thoughts. Perhaps reading a challenged book that deals with teen suicide in a productive way, like *Flamer* or *Forgive me, Leonard Peacock*, could address this topic in ways that help youth.

♦ Whether the parents and guardians of freshman want to admit it or not, many teens are sexually active in high school, and some have experienced nonconsensual sexual activity (Society for Adolescent Health and Medicine, 2023), so youth in their first year of high school need to hear unequivocally what is and what is not consent. Teen suicide rates have increased in recent years in the U.S.

(Jason Foundation, n.d.), and issues surrounding teen suicide also need to be addressed delicately and responsibly. It is a myth that talking about suicide encourages suicide (Jefferson Center, n.d.), and according to the 988 Suicide & Crisis Lifeline (formerly known as the National Suicide Prevention Lifeline; n.d.), asking someone if they are thinking about killing themselves in a nonjudgmental way can help them. Suicide is an important topic that should be talked about. Why not talk about it while reading a play that features it prominently?

- It is no secret that high school students often avoid completing assigned reading. This unit has the potential to motivate students to read an entire novel. While parents and guardians might disagree with some scenes or maybe even several chapters of a book, I think many would admit they'd be proud of their teen for reading an entire novel on their own.
- Based on national discourse and efforts to ban books focusing on characters who are members of LGBTQIA+ communities, I imagine many parents/guardians would not want their teens reading a book like *Flamer*, but according to a research brief developed by The Trevor Project (2023), LGBTQIA+ youth who interact with accepting adults are less likely to attempt suicide than their peers who did not have support from adults. Reading a book like *Flamer* could help LGBTQIA+ youth (whether they are out or not), who are more likely to experience suicidality than their peers (Trevor Project, 2023). It might help a concerned parent to know that *Flamer* is an option, not a required book, and that reading *Flamer* could help a student experiencing suicidal ideation.

Using many of these points, I've written an example letter you could send to parents or guardians to let them know about your plans for the R&J Issues Unit (see Appendix B). You are welcome to use the letter, but you will need to include the correct contact information.

Spend Time Reflecting

This concluding section is essentially the same in Chapters 5, 6, and 7 because the advice applies to all experiences of wobble caused from providing CLP. While I've discussed some moments of wobble I think you might experience if you teach for CHANGE with freshmen, each teacher experiences wobble in their own ways. Moments of wobble often produce feelings of fear, at least for me and the teachers I've studied. In his book *The Heart of the Buddha's Teaching: Transforming Suffering into Peace, Joy, and Liberation*, the late Buddhist monk and teacher Thich Nhat Hanh discusses the importance of mindfully acknowledging our feelings and letting them run through our minds without judgment. Hanh (2015) wrote, "when our feelings are stronger than our mindfulness, we suffer" (p. 73). If you're wobbling as you consider implementing a unit like the R&J Issues Unit for CHANGE, that's okay! Your wobble does not have to make you suffer. Take some time to reflect on what your feelings are telling you about your teaching practice and about yourself as a human. Look deeply into them, without judging yourself or allowing the feelings to take over. I hope you'll find that pausing and reflecting will give you perspective and produce wisdom that you can apply to your teaching practice.

Notes

1 Remember that teachers are mandatory reporters, so be prepared to report any abuse that students share with you. Make clear to students before the class discussion begins that you cannot promise you will not share what they say in class with the appropriate authorities. You may want to talk to your school counselors about potential resources they could suggest you make available to students.
2 I recommend that you collaborate with school counselors so they can offer you resources and support for a lesson addressing teen suicide. Please remind students that you are a mandatory reporter and that you care deeply for them.

References

988 Suicide & Crisis Lifeline. (n.d.). *How the 5 steps can help someone who is suicidal*. BeThe1To. https://www.bethe1to.com/bethe1to-steps-evidence/

Beck, V. S., & Boys, S. (2012). Romeo & Juliet: Star-crossed lovers or sex offenders? *Criminal Justice Policy Review, 24*(6), 655–675.

Daniels, H. (1994). *Literature circles: Voice and choice in literature circles and reading groups*. Stenhouse.

Dyches, J., Sams, B., & Boyd, A. S. (2020). *Acts of resistance: Subversive teaching the English language arts classroom*. Myers Education Press.

Garcia, A., & O'Donnell-Allen, C. (2015). *Pose, wobble, flow: A culturally proactive approach to literacy instruction*. Teachers College Press.

Goble, R. R., & Wiersum, E. (2019, March 21). *Epic explorations: Teaching the "Odyssey" with The New York Times*. New York Times. https://www.nytimes.com/2019/03/21/learning/lesson-plans/epic-explorations-teaching-the-odyssey-with-the-new-york-times.html

Hanh, T. N. (2015). *The heart of the Buddha's teaching: Transforming suffering into peace, joy, and liberation*. Harmony.

Harris, E. A., & Alter, A. (2023, September 21). *Book bans are rising sharply in public libraries*. New York Times. https://www.nytimes.com/2023/09/21/books/book-ban-rise-libraries.html

Hickson, M. (2022, October 31). *Opinion: The school library used to be a sanctuary. Now it's a battleground*. CNN. https://www.cnn.com/2022/10/31/opinions/school-libraries-banned-books-lgbtq-hickson/index.html

Janks, H. (2000). Domination, access, diversity, and design: A synthesis for critical literacy education. *Educational Review, 52*(2), 175–186.

Jason Foundation. (n.d.). Facts & stats. Retrieved September 28, 2023, from https://jasonfoundation.com/youth-suicide/facts-stats/

Jefferson Center. (n.d.). *The truth about three common suicide myths and how you can help someone in crisis*. https://www.jcmh.org/the-truth-about-three-common-suicide-myths-and-how-you-can-help-someone-in-crisis/

McLaughlin, E. C. (2022, June 4). *Book banning in the US: These are the authors of color who censors are trying to silence.* CNN. https://www.cnn.com/2022/06/04/us/banned-book-authors/index.html

McNary, A. Z., & Rodríguez, R. J. (2020). Reading *The Odyssey* today: Subversive outsiders, stances, and journeys. In J. Dyches, B. Sams, & A. S. Boyd (Eds.), *Acts of resistance: Subversive teaching in the English language arts classroom* (pp. 199–211). Myers Education Press.

Moje, E. B. (2008). Foregrounding the disciplines in secondary literacy teaching and learning: A call for change. *Journal of Adolescent & Adult Literacy, 52*(2), 96–107.

Moje, E. B. (2015). Doing and teaching disciplinary literacy with adolescent learners: A social and cultural enterprise. *Harvard Educational Review, 85*(2), 254–278.

Morrell, E. (2008). *Critical literacy and urban youth: Pedagogies of access, dissent, and liberation.* Routledge.

ProCon.org. (2024, January 29). *Banned books: Top 3 pros and cons.* Retrieved July 17, 2024, from https://www.procon.org/headlines/banned-books-top-3-pros-and-cons/

Rainey, E. C. (2017). Disciplinary literacy in English language arts: Exploring the social and problem-based nature of literary reading and reasoning. *Reading and Research Quarterly, 52*(1), 53–71.

Society for Adolescent Health and Medicine. (2023). Promoting sexual consent principles in the sexual and reproductive health care of adolescents and young adults. *Journal of Adolescent Health, 73*, 205–209. DOI: https://doi.org/10.1016/j.jadohealth.2023.04.002

Steiss, J. (2020). Dismantling winning stories: Lessons from applying critical literature pedagogy to *The Odyssey. Journal of Adolescent & Adult Literacy, 63*(4), 433–441. DOI: 10.1002/jaal.1012

The Trevor Project. (2023, September 22). *Research brief: Acceptance from adults is associated with lower rates of suicide attempts among LGBTQ young people.* https://www.thetrevorproject.org/research-briefs/acceptance-from-adults-is-associated-with-lower-rates-of-suicide-attempts-among-lgbtq-young-people-sep-2023/

White, J. (2016, March 15). *Parents shouldn't let schools force kids to read smut.* The Federalist. https://thefederalist.com/2016/03/15/parents-shouldnt-let-schools-force-kids-to-read-smut/

Literature Cited

Andrews, J. (2015). *Me and earl and the dying girl* (Revised edition). Amulet Books.

Curato, M. (2020). *Flamer*. Henry Holt & Company.

Hammonds, J. (2022). *We deserve monuments*. Roaring Brook Press.

Pérez, A. H. (2019). *Out of darkness*. Holiday House.

Quick, M. (2014). *Forgive me, Leonard peacock*. Little Brown, and Company.

Rowell, R. (2013). *Eleanor & park*. St. Martin's Griffin.

Shakespeare, W. (2012). *The Arden Shakespeare: Romeo & Juliet* (R. Weis, Ed.). Bloomsbury.

5

What Could Critical Literacy Pedagogy Look Like in Grade 10?

As professor and researcher Allan Luke (2012) explained, some of the foundational or "classical" questions of critical literacy are "What is 'truth'? How is it presented, by whom, and in whose interests?" (p. 4). Luke also pointed out that critical questions are "curriculum questions about whose version of culture, history, and everyday life will count as official knowledge" (p. 5). Professor and researcher Jeanne Dyches (2018) argued that curricula, through their inclusions and silences, can both "privilege" and "marginalize" certain perspectives and experiences (p. 237). Dyches advocated for critical literacy pedagogy (CLP) that "equips students with the literacies to understand textual representation, omissions, and silences" (p. 237). Curricular questions are questions of power and who has the power to decide whose perspectives are recognized and privileged and whose perspectives are silenced. English language arts (ELA) curricula in all grades in high school offer teachers and students opportunities to speak to, speak back to, and speak against the abuse of curricular power, but grade 10 curricula offer some unique possibilities.

Opportunities for Critical Literacy Pedagogy with Grade 10 Curriculum

ELA curricula for grade 10 vary from state to state and from school to school. While this might not be true for every grade 10 ELA curriculum, grade 10 curricula often use the study of literature, combined with related informational texts, to immerse students in exploring certain themes deemed relevant for adolescents (e.g., coming of age, dealing with change, navigating family relationships, identity, injustice, and personal growth).

Some of the main texts traditionally studied in grade 10 are the play *A Raisin in the Sun* by Lorraine Hansberry, the novel *To Kill a Mockingbird* by Harper Lee, and the memoir *Night* by Elie Wiesel. Hansberry's *A Raisin in the Sun* addresses topics related to family relationships, identity, personal growth, and injustice. Lee's *To Kill a Mockingbird* also addresses navigating family relationships, personal growth, and injustice as well as coming of age. Wiesel's memoir *Night* compels readers to explore the unfathomable injustice of the Holocaust. Some grade 10 curricula require the study of a Shakespearean play as well. Many of Shakespeare's plays address themes related to the topics listed above.

Because ELA curricula for grade 10 regularly organize themselves around these issues and themes, grade 10 ELA affords teachers excellent opportunities to enact CLP. First, you can replace canonical texts that address a theme with different, more diverse texts that address the same theme. If you're required to teach a particular book, you can comply with the mandate while teaching the text subversively to engage students in critical literacy (see Dyches et al., 2020).

Of course, not all texts often included in the grade 10 curriculum need to be replaced. *A Raisin in the Sun* comes to mind: I am not advocating that teachers cease studying this play with their students. Because it takes place in the 1950s, *A Raisin in the Sun* has, however, been taught in ways that treat anti-Black racism as a thing of the past. Obviously, the play can be taught critically to support students in speaking back to racial injustice that is occurring today. If you are required to teach this play, you can provide supplemental texts to teach for CHANGE. You may want to provide students with excerpts of *The Color of Law: A Forgotten History of How Our Government Segregated America* by Richard Rothstein (2018) that discuss Chicago's racist housing policies. The reality of these racist policies connects to the Black characters in the play who live in racially segregated Southside Chicago and pay higher prices for housing than White tenants. As Rothstein explained, intentional racial discrimination resulted in the exploitation of Black tenants in Chicago by White landlords. You could use Serrato and colleagues' (2022) interactive online article to help students investigate and visualize Chicago's past and current racial segregation. You and your students could research recent lawsuits against Wells Fargo Bank that accuse the bank of discriminatory lending practices against Black mortgage applicants in the 21st century (see Waters, 2022). Such supplemental texts could help your students read critically and investigate how racism still impacts Black people living in Chicago and cities across the United States today.

Many teachers do their best to use Lee's *To Kill a Mockingbird* (*TKAM*) to challenge the racism and the injustice that Tom Robinson experiences. If taught critically, *TKAM* can support students in speaking back to racism and injustices in society and policing. When I used to teach it, I asked students to survey their peers to identify examples of racism occurring at our school and to research possible solutions to the issues they discovered. The unit I taught attempted to get students to see that racism is not a thing of the past and to support students in Challenging injustice to Help make a difference by Asking and answering tough questions and Noticing ways to Get involved in and Engaged in making our school a better environment. My students did not have to read *TKAM* to participate in the unit, though. We could have done something similar even if we studied a different novel. We could have studied Angie Thomas's *The Hate U Give* (2017) or the prequel *Concrete Rose* (2021), for example.

While Lee's *TKAM* is a high school classic and beloved by many readers, it may be time to replace it. As stated above, most teachers use this novel to address issues of race and racism. Still, to many people, like professor and critical scholar Ibram

X. Kendi, *TKAM* is a "White savior" novel that emphasizes the actions and agency of the White characters and ignores the Black activism during 1930s when the novel takes place. Kendi (2017) argues that *TKAM* portrays Black characters as "waiting and hoping and singing for a White savior, and thankful for the moral heroism of lawyer Atticus Finch" (p. 370). This portrayal is what Kendi calls *TKAM's* "underlying racism" (p. 369). Because of the potentially harmful messages the novel can convey and because other novels address similar themes of coming of age, navigating family relationships, personal growth, and injustice, teachers seeking to implement CLP may want to replace it.

Of course, teachers may be required to teach *TKAM*. I was required to when I taught grade 10, so if you are planning to teach this novel soon, there are ways to do so subversively. First, and I'm sure you know this, use the book to challenge injustice today in the communities surrounding your school. As legislators continue to censor texts available in classrooms and schools and to try to silence critical discussions of race and racism (see Stout & Wilburn, 2022), I encourage you to persist in using *TKAM* to teach for CHANGE. Please continue to help students read the word and the world so they can recognize that racism is not stuck in the South in the 1930s. Racism is everywhere in the United States, right now.

As you explore current examples of racism, though, please provide students with supplemental readings to learn about Black people's past and current activism. As you're likely already doing when you teach this novel, teachers can pair Dr. Martin Luther King, Jr.'s "Letter from the Birmingham Jail" with the novel to emphasize Black activism in the 1960s, when the novel was published. Teachers may also consider including excerpts from Malcolm X's autobiography (Haley, 1989) to show a different approach to Black activism from Dr. King's use of nonviolence.

To address Black activism today against current racist actions and policies, teachers can help students navigate the Black Lives Matter (n.d.) website where they can find resources like suggested language for social media posts about the continued impact of Trayvon Martin's murder. Teachers and students can also explore the Black activism during the summer of 2020 following the tragic and criminal deaths of Breonna Taylor and George Floyd. The edited collection *Four Hundred Souls: A Community History of African America, 1619–2019* (Kendi & Blain, 2021) is a valuable resource that contains short essays on Black history and activism in the United States. You can provide supplemental informational texts for students to read from this collection of essays. A final suggestion for teaching *TKAM* for CHANGE is to support students in questioning the novel. You can tell them that as they study the text, they are to explore this question: Is this a White savior novel? Students could cite evidence supporting their claim, and they could produce arguments for or against the continued study of the novel.

Wiesel's memoir *Night* can also be used to promote critical literacy in grade 10 ELA classrooms. You can use this text to investigate abuses of power and to advocate against genocide and mass injustices around the globe. Still, as students in Dyches's (2018) study pointed out, if the study of genocide or mass injustice in school addresses only the Holocaust, harmful messages can be communicated to students. One student in Dyches's study pointed out that other large-scale injustices are not studied in school likely because of Eurocentricity, and another student said reading examples of mass injustice and genocide that solely focus on European nations "pushes a belief of White supremacy" (p. 243). Of course, I want to be careful here. I am not trying to diminish the Holocaust. Words do not exist to describe that injustice, and students should continue reading texts like *Night* in school. In her study, Dyches explained, however, that *Night* was the only required text in secondary curricula that addressed mass injustice. If a unit on injustice in grade 10 ELA focuses only on the Holocaust, it is possible that harmful messages are communicated to students.

Therefore, if you teach a unit on *Night* or injustice, you can promote critical literacy by supporting students in studying other examples of genocide and injustice as well as those perpetuated during the Holocaust. In Dyches's (2018) study, some of the other injustices students discussed and researched were women's rights in Colombia, the Armenian Genocide, and the Civil War in El Salvador. They also read excerpts of Michelle Alexander's (2012) book *The New Jim Crow: Mass Incarceration in the Age of Colorblindness* to discuss mass injustices in the United States, like those manifested by the "War on Drugs." Exploring more examples of genocide and mass injustice supported the students in Dyches's study in speaking back to power, specifically the curricular power to advance some perspectives and silence others.

For those required to teach Shakespeare in grade 10, remember you can teach Shakespearean plays critically. For example, professor Ashley K. Dallacqua collaborated with Annmarie Sheahan, a grade 10 ELA teacher, to decenter Shakespeare's *Hamlet* by supporting students in speaking back to curricular power that continues to privilege texts written by dead White men (Dallacqua & Sheahan, 2020; see also Sheahan & Dallacqua, 2020). Sheahan's school required her to teach *Hamlet* in grade 10, so Dallacqua and Sheahan used the study of the play to challenge curricular silences and investigate questions of power and privilege. Dallacqua and Sheahan paired *Hamlet* with Gregory Neri's (2010) graphic novel *Yummy: The Last Days of a Southside Shorty*, which tells the stories of the Black Disciples gang in Chicago in the 1990s, because both texts address themes related to the consequences of violence. Including the graphic novel allowed students to "take into account race, class, and the impact of privilege on the consequences of violence" (Sheahan & Dallacqua, 2020, p. 4) that reading *Hamlet* by itself could not afford. Their unit allowed students to critically analyze a canonical text and to expand their understanding of what should count as literature worthy of study. Any teacher who is required to teach Shakespeare can draw inspiration from their example.

Below, I'll describe a specific unit you can use to challenge curricular and historical silences. As Haitian scholar Michel-Rolph Trouillot (2015) explained, the word *history* can mean both "the facts of the matter and a narrative of those facts, both 'what happened' and 'that which is said to have happened'" (p. 2). Trouillot pointed out that a power differential exists that allows some narratives to spread while others are silenced. The suggested unit detailed below engages students in Challenging injustice to Help make a difference by Asking and answering tough questions and Noticing ways to Get involved and Engaged in making the world better. Specifically, this unit engages students in exploring how curricula and history can silence narratives and supports them in speaking back to and against this power so they can uplift previously silenced voices.

Overview of the Speaking into the Silence Unit for CHANGE

This suggested unit focuses on the study of Ibi Zoboi's (2017) young adult novel *American Street*. Zoboi was born in Port-au-Prince, Haiti, and as she writes in her personal essay about her identity, "Haitian Sensation" (2021), she tried, as a child growing up in Brooklyn, to deny the fact that she was Haitian. She wanted to assimilate, but as she grew older, she realized "identity has a way of calling you back to your true self" (p. 92). Part of what she describes as her "long journey" to celebrating her Haitian identity was learning about "the Haitian revolution, Vodou, and African History" (p. 94). Learning history and culture that had been silenced and ignored in school curricula sustained Zoboi on her journey to proudly proclaiming "I am Black. I am African. I am Haitian" (p. 97). As students study Zoboi's novel, they too will learn about previously silenced history and culture. They will also speak back to and against the power to silence so they can challenge the silences of traditional secondary ELA curricula. The unit objective is for students to research events or cultures that have been silenced and to create a project they will share with the school community documenting what they learned. You and your students can brainstorm topics for research, but here are some suggestions: Immigrant experiences in the United States (past and current), the internment of Japanese Americans during World War II, the Osage Murders (which have gained more attention because of Martin Scorsese's [2023] film *Killers of the Flower Moon* based on David Grann's [2018] excellent book),

Haitian Vodou, and examples of Black resistance to slavery in the U.S. (e.g., Denmark Vesey, who had been enslaved in Haiti and planned an insurrection in Charleston, South Carolina, in 1822 [see Jones, 2021], or Mary Bowser, a Black woman who spied on the Confederacy for the Union during the Civil War; listen to a podcast about Mary Bowser by Kumanyika and White [2018]).

I suggest that you collaborate with the school librarian or media center specialist to help your students conduct and record their research. You could require your students to create video essays, a multimodal form of digital composition, to convey what they learned through their research (see Kittle & Gallagher, 2021, for suggestions on teaching digital composition). You can also collaborate with other faculty and staff at your school to host an event, perhaps in the auditorium or school library, for your students to share their projects with an audience of community members. You may even want to work with a local library branch to host the public event there. Giving students a real audience for their projects imparts to them the agency they can have to give voice to something previously silenced. It shows them they can take actions for CHANGE.

Zoboi's novel *American Street* takes place in Detroit, Michigan, where the 16-year-old protagonist Fabiola Toussaint reconnects with her aunt and American cousins. At the beginning of the novel, Fabiola and her mother travel from Port-au-Prince, Haiti, to the United States. Fabiola is an American citizen because her mother gave birth to her while in the U.S., but Fabiola's mother is Haitian and is detained by Immigration. Throughout the entire novel, Fabiola hopes to be reunited with her mother as she navigates change, attempts to make sense of and realize her identity, negotiates family relationships, experiences romance and loss, and gains wisdom and self-understanding that come only from conquering hardships. *American Street* is a wonderful novel to study in a grade 10 ELA classroom because it addresses several of the themes that are often the focus of grade 10 instruction.

I suggest that you teach *American Street* instead of *To Kill a Mockingbird*. You may be able to receive funding to purchase a class set of novels from DonorsChoose, a 501(c)(3) not-for-profit corporation dedicated to supporting teachers in getting the resources they need (DonorsChoose, n.d.). To teach the lesson plans described below, you will want to make sure to give students some background information on Haiti; Haitian Vodou; Haitian Creole, which in "Haitian Sensation" Zoboi defines as "a mix of African, Indigenous, and French" languages (p. 96); and the city of Detroit.

Speaking into the Silence Unit Lesson Plans

These plans focus on critical aspects of the Unit. The main objective is for students to research a historical or curricular silence and create a project to end that silence. The first lesson plan is written as if you've already introduced students to the novel and have started teaching it.

Speaking into the Silence Unit Lesson Plan 1

When to implement this lesson:	After students have read and discussed the first five chapters of the novel
Lesson objective:	Students will investigate how the nations of the United States and Haiti have impacted each other.
Assessment:	In groups, students will generate a list of the ways the United States and Haiti have impacted each other. Individually, students will complete an "Exit Ticket" asking them to identify which information they already knew and anything new they learned. (This lesson is meant to help students notice things that have been silenced from history: Most students will have learned of the Louisiana Purchase, but how many of them know it was possible only because of the Haitian Revolution?)
Suggested texts needed:	The links to these texts are included in the references at the end of this chapter. ♦ "The Louisiana Purchase Was Driven by a Slave Rebellion" by Erin Blakemore (2023) ♦ "U.S. Invasion and Occupation of Haiti, 1915–34" (The Office of the Historian, n.d.-a) and "The United States and the Haitian Revolution, 1791–1804" (The Office of the Historian, n.d.-b) ♦ "'The Greatest Heist In History': How Haiti Was Forced to Pay Reparations for Freedom" by Greg Rosalsky (2021)

(Continued)

Suggested activities:	This lesson uses the Jigsaw Strategy. You will need to place students in two different groups during the lesson. One group, the Home Group, is the group responsible for listing how the two countries have impacted each other. This group can accomplish the assessment only after each member of the home group has had the opportunity to work with their Expert Group, which is made up of students from different Home Groups. Each Expert Group will be assigned a different text to read, so they each have a unique "piece of the jigsaw puzzle" to contribute to their Home Group. ♦ Start students in their Home Groups and support them in reading the article by Rosalsky. Help students connect one of the concerns of the article (e.g., the plight of Haitian refugees) to Fabiola and her mom's experiences in *American Street*. ♦ Then put students in their Expert Groups with new peers to read the three other articles. You will probably need more than three Expert Groups, so you can create six Expert Groups, and two will read the same article. In each Expert Group, students will learn (1) how U.S. leadership felt about the Haitian Revolution as it was happening, (2) how and why the U.S. invaded Haiti in the early 20th century, and (3) how the Haitian Revolution brought about the Louisiana Purchase and the influence that had on slavery in the United States. ♦ Once students have had time to learn from their groups' assigned articles in their Expert Groups, bring them back to their Home Groups and have them share what they learned so they can create their list of the ways these two nations impacted each other. ♦ Ask Home Groups to share their list and discuss with the class as time allows. ♦ Conclude the lesson with the "Exit Ticket" assignment.

Speaking into the Silence Unit Lesson Plan 2

When to implement this lesson:	Immediately after Lesson Plan 1
Lesson objectives:	Students will review what they learned in their Home and Expert Groups from Lesson Plan 1, consider different opinions on the power of history and curricula to silence, and participate in a class discussion.

(Continued)

Assessment:	Students will record their ideas in response to several prompts and use these notes to participate in a class discussion.
Suggested texts needed:	No texts needed

Suggested activities:	♦ To help students gather their thoughts before a larger, whole-class discussion, begin with a brief discussion activity. Label each wall or corner of the room as one of the following: strongly agree, agree, disagree, and strongly disagree. Then display several open-ended statements (see suggested statements below) that could spark discussion. Ask students to consider each prompt and move to the wall or corner that most represents how they feel. Then have students discuss their thoughts with each other in their chosen location. Next, have each group share their views with the class. Give students time to consider if they want to stay in their first location or switch to another. Invite more discussion and move on to the next prompt. The suggested prompts are meant to prepare students to discuss the topic of historical and curricular silencing:
	   ○ "If something happened a hundred years ago, it can't really impact things today much. It's the past."
	   ○ "History books can't cover everything that happened, so it's fine that they don't tell us some things."
	   ○ "Studying history should focus only on facts that have been recorded."
	   ○ "I was surprised by some things we learned recently about how Haiti's history impacted the United States."
	♦ Once students have shared and potentially reconsidered their initial positions, share with them the following quotes/ideas from Trouillot's book *Silencing the Past: Power and the Production of History*:
	   ○ "History means both the facts of the matter and a narrative of those facts, both 'what happened' and 'that which is said to have happened'" (p. 2).
	   ○ Who gets to narrate what happened is a question of power.
	   ○ The discipline of Social Studies in the United States has silenced the Haitian Revolution: Trouillot stated, "[History] has taught generations of readers that the period from 1776 to 1843 should be called 'The Age of Revolution.' At the very same time, this corpus has remained silent on the most radical political revolution of that age [i.e., the Haitian Revolution]" (2015, p. 98).

(Continued)

- ♦ Ask students to spend five minutes writing their responses to each of these points. Encourage students to identify if they agree or disagree with each statement and why. Require them to use something they learned from Lesson Plan 1 as support for their responses. Also require students to use something from *American Street* as support for their points. (Students may notice that Fabiola's cousins have an inaccurate understanding of Haitian Vodou, even though their mother used to practice it.)
- ♦ Then begin the large, whole-class discussion focusing on the topic of historical and curricular silencing. You may want to use the following prompts to keep the discussion going:
  - What are some things your social studies textbooks have silenced?
  - How do you think things can be silenced in an English language arts class?
  - Why do you think Fabiola's cousins had such negative experiences in elementary school in *American Street* (see "Princess's Story")?
  - How do Fabiola's first few experiences in the United States relate to the idea of historical and curricular silencing?
- ♦ Even though I know you know how to lead class discussions, I like to share my suggestions in case you find them helpful:
  - Remind students of class rules and norms.
  - Print out example sentence starters and tape them to each student's desk so they can practice using the discourse valued in respectful discussions. For example, I might use some sentence starters they can use to participate in scholarly discourse. To help students state their opinion and defend it with evidence, they could use this sentence starter: "The author suggests [blank.] Notice what they wrote on page [blank]." To help students disagree respectfully, they could use this sentence starter: "That is one perspective, but I have a different one. What if we view it this way: [blank]?" To keep the discussion going, students could use this sentence starter: "What other perspectives are there, or who has something to say but has not been able to yet?"
  - If time allows, have students reflect on their participation in the concluded discussion by answering questions like "How did I contribute to the class discussion? Did I contribute mostly by being a good listener, or did I contribute verbally or virtually to the discussion?" and "What would I do differently the next time we have a discussion?"

Speaking into the Silence Unit Lesson Plan 3

When to implement this lesson:	Immediately after Lesson Plan 2
Lesson objectives:	♦ Students will find two specific ways the Haitian Revolution impacted the history of the United States (i.e., the Haitian Revolution influenced the passing of the 1793 Fugitive Slave Act and inspired Black people in the U.S. to rebel against slavery), and they will discuss why the Haitian Revolution is relatively silenced in their social studies classes. ♦ Students will analyze an essay to determine the author's purpose.
Assessment:	Students will respond to this prompt: *What is Owens's purpose for writing this essay? Identify two statements made by Owens that you think provide clues to their purpose.*
Suggested text needed:	The book chapter "1794–1799: The Fugitive Slave Act" by Deirdre Cooper Owens (2021), from the edited collection of essays *Four Hundred Souls: A Community History of African America, 1619–2019*
Suggested activities:	♦ When you introduce the book chapter to students, let them know it comes from a collection of essays put together by people who wanted to highlight Black voices and Black experiences in the United States. ♦ Have students create T-charts to use as they read the essay. On the left side, they are to record historical facts. On the right side, they are to record the author's narrative or interpretation of those facts. Students should work in pairs to complete their charts. ♦ Support students in completing their chart. ♦ After the pairs of students have read the essay and completed their chart, they should join another pair near them to form a group of four students. ♦ Before assigning them their new group task, discuss with students how the author's narrative of facts implies their interpretation of those facts. Then ask them as a group to discuss what they learned from reading the essay as well as the author's purpose for their essay. ♦ Have each student respond to the prompt from the assessment section, and as time allows, encourage students to share their responses with the class.

Speaking into the Silence Unit Lesson Plan 4

When to implement this lesson:	Immediately after Lesson 3
Lesson objectives:	♦ Students will participate in a class discussion to list, group, and label potential topics to research for their projects. ♦ Students will begin researching their chosen topic.
Assessment:	Students should have a topic selected by the end of the lesson.
Suggested texts needed:	Students will need access to the internet to begin researching their selected topics.
Suggested activities:	♦ Begin the lesson by reviewing the concept of historical and curricular silencing. Help them recognize that the silencing of Haiti's history can make Haiti seem unimportant, which could make someone from Haiti feel unimportant. ♦ Introduce the unit project to the class. Let them know that they will research a topic they do not know much about because it has been silenced, ignored, or left out of their schooling until now. ♦ Give students a few minutes to do preliminary research online about historical or curricular silences they could research. ♦ Then have students brainstorm with a partner or small groups to discuss what topics they are considering researching. ♦ Next, ask the pairs or small groups for suggestions. Record their ideas somehow, perhaps on a white board or projected for the whole class to see. ♦ After several topics have been listed, ask students to help you group them into categories. They may be grouped by a specific type of injustice, like discrimination based on genders or sexualities or genocide. They might be grouped by type of silencing (i.e., historical versus curricular). ♦ Once the list has been categorized into groups, have students help you label the groups. This helps students see how the groups are related. It also helps them see the need to narrow their topic. ♦ Finally, support students for the rest of class in researching their topic.

Speaking into the Silence Unit Lesson Plan 5

When to implement this lesson:	After students have read and discussed the first nine chapters of the novel
Lesson objectives:	♦ Students will read two sources about another historical and curricular silence to identify how redlining practices contributed to racial segregation and inequalities in Detroit. ♦ Students will analyze how the author developed their central idea in these two sources and will list evidence the author used to support their central idea.
Assessment:	Students will take notes identifying the author's central idea and will document evidence the author used to support their points. Students will use these notes to participate in a class discussion.
Suggested texts needed:	♦ Two online articles posted on Michigan State University's Extension website by Assistant Professor Dr. Craig Wesley Carpenter. The links to the articles "Detroit" (n.d.-a) and "Redlining in Michigan: The History and Legacy of Racist Housing Policies" (n.d.-b) are included in the references at the end of this chapter under Carpenter. ♦ If students are interested in researching redlining in their area for their unit project, you may want to share this online interactive map of redlining in the United States, provided by Nelson et al. (2023): https://dsl.richmond.edu/panorama/redlining/ Students can select "Explore the Maps" and then search a city to further their research. The website includes pages with suggestions for teaching about redlining, which could help you and your students explore this topic further together.
Suggested activities:	♦ Introduce the lesson by giving students a purpose for reading: Tell students that in this lesson they are going to read about an injustice that took place in Detroit, Michigan, that has largely been silenced until now. ♦ In pairs, have students read "Redlining in Michigan: The History and Legacy of Racist Housing Policies" first. Tell them to read to define redlining and explain the impact of redlining on people of color in the United States. ♦ Then have students read "Detroit." Tell them to read to identify the author's central idea expressed in both articles. ♦ As time allows, engage in a class discussion of redlining and how it shaped what modern Detroit, the Detroit Fabiola lives in, looks like today.

Speaking into the Silence Unit Lesson Plan 6

When to implement this lesson:	Immediately after Lesson 5
Lesson objectives:	Students will research Haitian Vodou and compare what it is with the way it is often represented in media.
Assessment:	Students will write letters to Fabiola, telling her what they have learned recently about Haiti and Haitian Vodou.
Suggested texts needed:	♦ The video titled "How 'Voodoo' Became a Metaphor for Evil," produced by Josh Toussaint-Strauss (2020) ♦ Polyné and McAlister's (2017) article titled "Haiti and the Distortion of Vodou" published by CNN The links to the video and article are in references at the end of this chapter.
Suggested activities:	♦ Start the lesson by asking students to share ways they have seen Vodou represented in the media. Record and display their responses so the class can see. ♦ Then ask students if the way it is depicted in *American Steet* matches what they have seen previously. ♦ Next, play the video "How 'Voodoo' Became a Metaphor for Evil." ♦ After the video, engage the class in a quick discussion of what they learned from viewing it. ♦ Then have students read the article by Polyné and McAlister. ♦ Conclude the lesson by giving students time to write their letters to Fabiola.

Speaking into the Silence Unit Lesson Plan 7

When to implement this lesson:	After students have read and discussed Chapter 14 of the novel
Lesson objectives:	♦ Students will read a personal essay to discuss its central ideas. ♦ Students will identify how aspects of Ibi Zoboi's life connect to Fabiola's experiences in *American Street*.
Assessment:	Students will compare Fabiola's character from the novel with Zoboi's experiences.
Suggested text needed:	Zoboi's (2021) personal essay, "Haitian Sensation"

(Continued)

Suggested activities:	♦ Begin the lesson by asking students to share what they know about Fabiola's character from the novel. Record and display their responses. Help them focus on aspects of Fabiola's identity. Ask questions about how she feels about being Haitian and an immigrant, even though she is American by birth. ♦ Introduce Zoboi's essay. Tell students that it is from a collection of personal essays about identity and that the purpose of the collection was to highlight the voices of women authors who were previously silenced. ♦ Have students read the essay and, as they read, encourage them to take note of what they learn about Zoboi's life. ♦ After students have read the essay, engage the class in a quick discussion of how Zoboi's essay connects to the novel and some of the things they have studied recently. ♦ Then move the discussion to Zoboi's central idea. In this essay, Zoboi discusses initially denying her "Haitianness" only to embrace it later in life. Ask students to discuss what made Zoboi initially deny her "Haitianness" and what makes her claim it with pride today. ♦ Conclude the lesson by asking students to create a Venn diagram comparing and contrasting Zoboi and her character Fabiola.

Speaking into the Silence Unit Lesson Plan 8

When to implement this lesson:	After students have read and discussed Chapter 24 of the novel
Lesson objectives:	♦ Students will reread Ibi Zoboi's personal essay "Haitian Sensation" to analyze how she uses both expressive and reflective writing to convey her main points. ♦ Students will participate in a class discussion of how authors can use personal reflection and expression to speak into silences.
Assessment:	Students will annotate Zoboi's essay by highlighting portions of the piece in which she uses expressive writing and portions in which she primarily uses reflective writing to make her points. Students will use their annotations to participate in a class discussion of the essay and how authors can speak into silences.

(Continued)

Suggested texts needed:	♦ Zoboi's (2021) personal essay, "Haitian Sensation" ♦ You may want to use writing exercises from Kelly Gallagher's (2011) book *Write Like This: Teaching Real-World Writing Through Modeling & Mentor Texts* to support students in this lesson and the next one.

Suggested activities:	♦ Projecting their definitions on the board, help students see how expressive and reflective writing are similar but slightly different. Display these points from Gallagher (2011), whose book inspired this lesson:
	   ○ Expressive writing is when "the writer shares thoughts, ideas, feelings, and questions about [their] experiences" (p. 25). It is personal writing the writer uses to tell the reader how they feel about a topic.
	   ○ Reflective writing is also personal, but it moves "beyond recounting an experience" into "an exploration of how that particular experience has shaped the writer" (p. 25). It is "a vehicle for exploring and discovering new thoughts" as the writer "looks at the past as a means of looking at the future" (p. 25).
	♦ Tell students that their task is to annotate the essay as they reread it to identify moments when Zoboi is primarily using expressive writing and moments when she is primarily using reflective writing.
	♦ Model for students how to differentiate between the two types of writing and then have them reread and annotate the rest of the essay.
	♦ Then engage the students in a class discussion about how Zoboi used expressive and reflective writing to speak into specific silences, like how power is often associated with a person's proximity to "whiteness," which is a term for the qualities, benefits, value, and privileges that because of racism and discrimination pertain to or are assumed to belong to White people but are denied to people of color (Delgado & Stefancic, 2017).

Speaking into the Silence Unit Lesson Plan 9

When to implement this lesson:	Immediately after Lesson Plan 8
Lesson objective:	Students will write a personal essay, using Ibi Zoboi's essay "Haitian Sensation" as a model, to express and reflect on important aspects of their identities.
Assessment:	Students' personal essays should include moments of expressive and reflective writing to communicate main ideas about important aspects of their identities.

(Continued)

Suggested text needed:	Zoboi's (2021) "Haitian Sensation"
Suggested activities:	♦ Tell students that using personal writing to speak into silences is one way they can advocate for CHANGE. Display for the class this quote from critical scholar and educator Paulo Freire (1970/2018): "To speak a true word is to transform the word" (p. 87). Engage students in a quick discussion about how that statement can be true—help them make connections to *American Street* and Zoboi's essay. ♦ Encourage students to brainstorm things about their identities they would like to explore more through expressive and reflective writing. ♦ Support students in their brainstorming, drafting, and revising their personal essays. ♦ Require students to highlight or otherwise identify moments in their writing when they are mostly using expressive writing and moments when they are mostly using reflective writing.

Speaking into the Silence Unit Lesson Plan 10[1]

When to implement this lesson:	After students have finished reading and discussing the novel
Lesson objectives:	Students will analyze the characters in *American Street* to participate in a class discussion and write a letter to a character of their choice.
Assessment:	Students will write a letter to the character of their choice, explaining how they understand the character, their motivations, and their actions.
Suggested texts needed:	♦ *American Street* ♦ You may want to use suggestions from Cardoza and Schneider's (2021) NPR article about teens' experiences with abusive relationships if students decide to focus on Donna or Dray. The link to the article is found in the references at the end of this chapter.
Suggested activities:	♦ Introduce the lesson by reminding students what they've learned about the construction of history: History is made by both what happened and what is *said* to have happened. This is how silences occur, either because what happened is ignored or because what is said to have happened distorts or otherwise silences what occurred. Connect this to the characters in the novel. Tell them the novel lets readers know what happened with the characters, but it also suggests what some people (i.e., the police or media) would *say* about the events and characters in the novel.

(*Continued*)

	<ul><li>Engage students in a class discussion of the characters. Start with things other people, like judgmental adults or the authorities, might say about them. For example, what would people in authority say about Fabiola's cousins selling drugs or Kasim, who sells drugs for Dray? What would they say about Donna's attention-seeking behavior?</li><li>Then have students refer to the novel to see what the novel tells readers about these characters. Have students discuss what else could be said about them to speak into silences or distortions of them.</li><li>Finally, have students select a character to whom they will write a letter. Their letters should explain to the character how the students understand the character and their motivations.</li></ul>

Anticipated Moments of Wobble with the Speaking into the Silence Unit

Teaching this unit may cause wobble because it highlights realities that are often silenced. Investigating redlining in Detroit and supporting students individually as they research other events or cultures that have been silenced could likely cause wobble because some people might interpret your decisions as "teaching Critical Race Theory" (CRT). As mentioned in Chapter 2, CRT is an academic field that investigates how the legal system in the U.S. continues to create and uphold racist structures in society (Delgado & Stefancic, 2017), and many states have passed laws restricting classroom discourse on issues surrounding race and racism (Stout & Wilburn, 2022). Depending on which state you teach in, "teaching CRT" may be illegal, and if so, I imagine this unit could cause you some serious wobble. You also might experience tension, dread, or doubt because the characters use a lot of profanity, Fabiola has sex for the first time, Fabiola's cousins sell drugs, Donna's boyfriend is an abusive drug dealer, and Fabiola's boyfriend Kasim is killed by police, which sparks protests.

Anticipated Moments of Wobble with Specific Lesson Plans
The first two lesson plans introduce the concept of historical and curricular silences and help students recognize that these silences

are not accidental but rather intentionally created to promote a narrative about what happened, a narrative that makes the United States seem morally superior to other nations. These lessons challenge some of the dominant messages about American exceptionalism. I imagine teaching them could cause some wobble as you might anticipate pushback from parents, guardians, and students. You might even anticipate being accused of "teaching CRT" in these lessons. Unfortunately, some of the recent restrictive policies meant to address CRT call for teachers to face disciplinary actions, including termination, if they teach that racism is ongoing or refuse to celebrate the "Founding Fathers" as heroes (see Colarossi, 2021). One way to address this wobble is to try to emphasize historical facts as much as possible instead of offering your interpretation of these facts. It is also helpful to remember that your lessons help students notice the difference between a historical fact and the narration of that fact. Even people who interpret history differently than I do have to admit that history involves interpretation. Helping students see that encourages them to think for themselves.

The suggested text for the third lesson comes from a collection of essays written by authors who were likely influenced by CRT. The authors of those chapters use their writing to push back against the way Black history has been taught in the United States. The potential for you to be accused of "teaching CRT" is high if you teach this lesson. While this anticipated wobble is a very real concern, I want to suggest that you tell students that history is a matter of both what occurred and what people *say* occurred (i.e., interpretation of the facts). If you teach this lesson, tell your students that Owens's (2021) essay narrates the facts from a particular perspective. Such instruction helps students think about the historical facts for themselves because it makes clear to them that what they are reading includes interpretation as well as documented facts.

The fifth lesson plan, like the first three, might cause some anticipatory wobble regarding the accusation that you are "teaching CRT." Researching redlining obviously highlights systematic racism in the past, but this lesson also encourages students to consider how those past racist policies continue to impact society today. Again, I believe emphasizing to students that understanding history involves studying what happened as well as people's interpretations of what happened can alleviate some of this wobble.

The sixth lesson plan, as the unit does, promotes a critical perspective of history and curricula. Critically examining how Haitian Vodou has been represented in the U.S. could cause some wobble, I imagine, for two reasons: First, you may, yet again, anticipate accusations of "teaching CRT." Second, you may anticipate accusations that you are imposing religion upon students by having them learn about Haitian Vodou. As you know, many texts studied in ELA classrooms were written from Christian perspectives, so students have always studied religion, at least a little, to understand these allusions. In *To Kill a Mockingbird*, Scout and Jem attend a Christian church service, so addressing religion as it relates to a text is nothing new in ELA. Helping your students understand Fabiola's religious practices is no different than what often occurs in ELA classrooms.

Lesson Plans 7, 8, and 9, like most of the suggested lesson plans, will likely cause some wobble as you may fear being accused of "teaching CRT." Zoboi's essay "Haitian Sensation" discusses whiteness and how some of her classmates in elementary school were perceived as being closer to their White teacher in terms of the color of their skin, eyes, and hair. Their closeness to whiteness bestowed power to them that Zoboi could not obtain. Whiteness is a tenet of CRT (Delgado & Stefancic, 2017). Some students, parents and guardians, and administrators might immediately reject the study of "Haitian Sensation" because it mentions "whiteness." The lessons I wrote are designed to help students recognize expressive and reflective writing so they can make connections with the author of *American Street* and so they can produce their own reflective and expressive writing. The lessons are not designed to force students to adopt an "anti-American" stance or to force them to accept tenets of CRT: This essay is a model of how to write expressively and reflectively. No personal writing will be devoid of biases and ideologies. Students do not have to agree with Zoboi to practice their own personal writing.

The final suggested lesson plan may cause you some wobble because students may wish to discuss Dray and Donna's abusive relationship, and this lesson asks students to tell a more comprehensive and compassionate story about the characters than what some people would feel the characters deserve. You may, therefore, anticipate being accused of championing drug dealers and of promoting an anti-police attitude. Encouraging students to broaden their perspectives and demonstrate empathy and compassion, though, is something most ELA teachers regularly do already. Therefore, while this may cause you some wobble, I think you can be comforted to know that this kind of instruction is something that many ELA teachers have valued for decades.

Encouragement to Expand Your Stretchiness

If you have experienced some wobble when considering teaching this unit, I offer suggestions for expanding your stretchiness so you can teach this unit even though it is causing you some tension, uncertainty, or discomfort. In general, my suggestions are the same for each recommended unit for grades 9, 10, 11, and 12. Those general suggestions are that you (1) collaborate with your English teacher peers, school administrators, and parents and guardians; (2) adjust the unit as needed; (3) create a rationale you can use to defend your pedagogical decisions; and (4) spend some time reflecting on what your discomfort can tell you about your teaching practice and your needs as a human and teacher.

Collaborate with Your English Teacher Peers, School Administrators, and Parents/Guardians

Work with the other grade 10 ELA teachers so that together you can adjust the suggested lesson plans as needed. You can also collaborate to create a rationale to defend your pedagogical decisions or revise the recommended letter to parents and guardians I've included in the Appendices (see Appendix C). I believe your experiences with wobble will be easier for you if you collaborate with your peers.

As a team, you can meet with your administrators to help them understand what you plan to do in class and the value of those plans. That way, they can feel equipped to support you in case a parent or guardian complains or accuses you of "teaching

CRT." You can also ask them for support during this meeting, which is much more easily gained before an issue arises than after.

I do not want to represent all parents and guardians as teachers' enemies. As I've documented, though, fear of parent or guardian complaints was the issue that caused the most wobble for the teachers in my study. This is a real concern for many teachers, but parents and guardians can be excellent allies as well. They care about their children and want them to learn. Communicating with them about what you're doing in the classroom can get them "on your side," which will reduce your experiences with wobble and will be better for your students because they will have support at home with assignments and their project.

Adjust the Unit

As discussed in previous chapters, Garcia & O'Donnell-Allen (2015) compared wobble to practicing yoga. When a yoga practitioner decides to try a pose, they may wobble because the required muscles are not strong enough yet to meet the demands of the pose. To continue practicing yoga, they need to respond to the wobble by making slight adjustments to the pose so they can keep attempting it, even if they can't perform the pose "perfectly." This metaphor applies to the Speaking into the Silence Unit. Adjust the unit (i.e., the metaphorical pose) slightly, and in time, you may feel stretchy enough to accomplish it as described in this chapter.

You could adjust the unit by removing some of the suggested informational texts, like "Haitian Sensation" and Owens's (2021) essay about the Fugitive Slave Act. Studying those texts with students increases the likelihood of your being accused of "teaching CRT." If that is a real concern for you because of state laws or district policies where you teach, please consider making this adjustment while still teaching *American Street* and supporting students in researching an event or culture that has been silenced.

Create a Rationale

If you decide to use the Speaking into the Silence Unit, you will probably benefit from preparing a rationale. In my study, Mrs. Skipmann benefitted from creating a rationale. She anticipated wobble because she planned to teach critical literacy theories like Marxism and feminism, so, as she said, she created a rationale "to cover [her] butt." This helped Mrs. Skipmann expand her stretchiness for wobble, and creating a rationale may do the same for you. As you prepare your rationale, I recommend that you also imitate Mr. Tophill and think about your teaching philosophy and what you feel is most important in ELA instruction. This reflection can guide you as you plan your rationale. Here are some points and suggestions I think could help you defend your decision to implement the Speaking into the Silence Unit:

- Regarding the concern that you may be accused of "teaching CRT," you can defend your decision to teach this unit and address racism by pointing out that the National Council of Teachers of English (NCTE), a leading professional organization dedicated to supporting ELA teachers and promoting excellent ELA instruction, maintains that educators have a right and a responsibility to provide antiracist teaching. NCTE has written a position statement titled, "Educators' Right and Responsibilities to Engage in Antiracist Teaching" (NCTE, 2022), which you may want to read and cite as you create your rationale. I hope you can feel comforted knowing that teaching lessons which address racism is considered by the NCTE to be your responsibility as an ELA teacher. This might help you convince administrators that you are fulfilling your professional duties by teaching this unit.
- Regarding the profanity in the novel *American Street*, I assume that many adolescents are used to hearing "fuck" and other profanity at school. If I were to teach this unit, I would create an anonymous survey asking students about their exposure to and comfort with hearing profanity. I might ask "How many times a day at school do you hear profanity at school?" as well as "How many times a day at school do you use profanity?" I bet those numbers are high, higher than many parents or guardians would like. Then I would share that data with administrators and parents and guardians in my letter to them.

This could be useful in supporting the decision to teach *American Street*, which includes a lot of profanity.
- Regarding Fabiola's decision to have sex with Kasim in the novel, as I wrote in the previous chapter, whether parents or guardians want to admit it or not, teens are sexually active in high school (Society for Adolescent Health and Medicine, 2023). *American Street* does not describe any sex acts, so it is unlikely that adolescents will read anything in this novel they are already not aware of.
- There is some other content in the novel that may cause wobble, like Donna and Dray's abusive relationship, the fact that Fabiola's cousins sell drugs, and Kasim's death at the hands of police. Of course, these are heavy topics that should be addressed delicately in the classroom. If you decide to create a survey before teaching this unit, I also recommend that you ask questions about the media that students consume. I imagine that most of them have streamed shows or movies about drug dealers, and the reality of police brutality against people of color is almost assuredly nothing new for students in schools today. Sadly, as Cardoza and Schneider (2021) stated, "26% of women say they experienced intimate partner violence before they were 18" (para. 1). Because teens can experience abusive relationships, there is value in addressing this real issue in a supportive environment.

Using some of the rationale points above, I've written an example letter you could send to parents and guardians and included it in the Appendices (see Appendix C). While you are welcome to use the letter in its entirety, you will need to add the correct contact information and data from your class survey.

Spend Time Reflecting

This concluding section is essentially the same in Chapters 4, 5, 6, and 7 because the advice applies to all experiences of wobble caused from teaching for CHANGE: While I've discussed some moments of wobble I think you might experience if you implement

CLP with sophomores, you'll experience wobble in your own way. Moments of wobble often produce feelings of fear. In his book *The Heart of the Buddha's Teaching: Transforming Suffering into Peace, Joy, and Liberation*, the late Buddhist monk and teacher Thich Nhat Hanh discusses the importance of mindfully acknowledging our feelings and letting them run through our minds without judgment. Hanh (2015) wrote, "when our feelings are stronger than our mindfulness, we suffer" (p. 73). If you're wobbling as you consider implementing this unit, that's okay! Your wobble does not have to make you suffer. Take some time to reflect on what your feelings are telling you about your teaching practice and about yourself as a human. Look deeply into them, without judging yourself or allowing the feelings to take over. I hope you'll find that pausing and reflecting will give you perspective and produce wisdom that you can apply to your teaching practice.

Note

1 Because this lesson might include conversations about abusive relationships, you will want to remind students that you are a mandatory reporter. I also suggest that you collaborate with school counselors to have resources available to share with students.

References

Alexander, M. (2012). *The new Jim Crow: Mass incarceration in the age of Colorblindness*.

Black Lives Matter. (n.d.). *About black lives matter*. https://blacklivesmatter.com/about/#vision

Blakemore, E. (2023, August 21). *The Louisiana purchase was driven by a slave rebellion*. History. https://www.history.com/news/louisiana-purchase-price-french-colonial-slave-rebellion

Cardoza, K., & Schneider, C. M. (2021, June 21). *Millions of teens experience abusive relationships. Here's how adults can help: Life kit*. NPR. https://www.npr.org/2021/05/06/994256485/abusive-relationships-teen-dating-violence-parents

Carpenter, C. W. (n.d.-a). *Detroit*. MSU Extension: Redlining in Michigan. https://www.canr.msu.edu/redlining/detroit

Carpenter, C. W. (n.d.-b). *Redlining in Michigan*. MSU Extension: Redlining in Michigan. https://www.canr.msu.edu/redlining/

Colarossi, N. (2021, October 2). *School board passes code to punish teachers over critical race theory after funding threat*. Newsweek. Retrieved October 11, 2021, from https://www.newsweek.com/school-board-passes-code-punish-teachersover-critical-race-theory-after-funding-threat-1635021

Dallacqua, A. K., & Sheahan, A. (2020). Making space: Complicating a canonical text through critical multimodal work in a secondary language arts classroom. *Journal of Adolescent & Adult Literacy, 64*(1), 67–77.

Delgado, R., & Stefancic, J. (2017). *Critical race theory: An introduction* (3rd ed.). NYU Press.

DonorsChoose. (n.d.). *Teacher sign-up*. https://www.donorschoose.org/teachers

Dyches, J. (2018). Investigating curricular injustices to uncover the injustices of curricula: Curriculum evaluation as critical disciplinary literacy practice. *The High School Journal, 101*(4), 236–250. https://doi.org/10.1353/hsj.2018.0013

Dyches, J., Sams, B., & Boyd, A. S. (2020). *Acts of resistance: Subversive teaching the English language arts classroom*. Myers Education Press.

Freire, P. (2018). *Pedagogy of the oppressed*. Bloomsbury. (Original work published in 1970).

Gallagher, K. (2011). *Write like this: Teaching real-world writing through modeling & mentor texts*. Stenhouse Publishers.

Garcia, A., & O'Donnell-Allen, C. (2015). *Pose, wobble, flow: A culturally proactive approach to literacy instruction*. Teachers College Press.

Grann, D. (2018). *Killers of the flower moon: The Osage murders and the birth of the FBI*. Vintage.

Hanh, T. N. (2015). *The heart of the Buddha's teaching: Transforming suffering into peace, joy, and liberation*. Harmony.

Haley, A. (1989). *The autobiography of Malcolm X: As told to Alex Haley*. Ballantine Books.

Jones, R. (2021). 1819–1824: Denmark Vesey. In I. X. Kendi & K. N. Blain (Eds.), *Four Hundred Souls: A Community History of African America, 1619–2019* (pp. 187–190). One World.

Kendi, I. X. (2017). *Stamped from the beginning: The definitive history of racist ideas in America*. Bold Type Books.

Kendi, I. X., & Blain, K. N. (Eds.). (2021). *Four hundred souls: A community history of African America, 1619–2019*. One World.

Kittle, P., & Gallagher, K. (2021). *4 essential studies: Beliefs and practices to reclaim student agency*. Heinemann.

Kumanyika, C., & White, K. C. (Hosts). (2018, November 9). The ring [Audio podcast episode]. In *Uncivil*. Gimlet Media. https://gimletmedia.com/shows/uncivil/39hw6e/the-ring

Luke, A. (2012). Critical literacy: Foundational notes. *Theory into Practice, 51*(4), 4–11. https://doi.org/10.1080/00405841.2012.636324

National Council of Teachers of English. (2022, September 8). *Educators' right and responsibilities to engage in antiracist teaching*. https://ncte.org/statement/antiracist-teaching/

Nelson, R. K., Winling, L., et al. (2023). *Mapping Inequality: Redlining in New Deal America*. Digital Scholarship Lab. https://dsl.richmond.edu/panorama/redlining

The Office of the Historian. (n.d.-a). *U.S. Invasion and occupation of Haiti, 1915–34*. State.gov. https://history.state.gov/milestones/1914-1920/haiti

The Office of the Historian. (n.d.-b). *The United States and the Haitian Revolution, 1791–1804*. State.gov. https://history.state.gov/milestones/1784-1800/haitian-rev

Owens, D. C. (2021). 1794–1799: The Fugitive Slave Act. In I. X. Kendi & K. N. Blain (Eds.), *Four hundred souls: A community history of African America, 1619–2019* (p. 162–165). One World.

Polyné, M., & McAlister, E. (2017, April 19). *Haiti and the distortion of Vodou*. CNN. https://www.cnn.com/2017/03/17/opinions/believer-haiti-vodou-polyne-mcalister/index.html

Rosalsky, G. (2021, October 5). *"The greatest heist in history": How Haiti was forced to pay reparations for freedom*. NPR. https://www.npr.org/sections/money/2021/10/05/1042518732/-the-greatest-heist-in-history-how-haiti-was-forced-to-pay-reparations-for-freed

Rothstein, R. (2018). *The color of law: A forgotten history of how our government segregated America*. Liveright Publishing.

Scorsese, M. (Director). (2023). *Killers of the flower moon [Film]*. Paramount Pictures.

Serrato, J., Runes, C., & Sier, P. (2022, February 24). *Mapping Chicago's racial segregation*. South Side Weekly. https://southsideweekly.com/mapping-chicagos-racial-segregation/

Sheahan, A., & Dallacqua, A. K. (2020). Taking scissors to Shakespeare. *Journal of Language & Literacy Education*, *16*(2), 1–13.

Society for Adolescent Health and Medicine. (2023). Promoting sexual consent principles in the sexual and reproductive health care of adolescents and young adults. *Journal of Adolescent Health*, *73*, 205–209. DOI: https://doi.org/10.1016/j.jadohealth.2023.04.002

Stout, C., & Wilburn, T. (2022, February 1). *CRT Map: Efforts to restrict teaching racism and bias have multiplied across the U.S.* Chalkbeat. https://www.chalkbeat.org/22525983/map-critical-race-theory-legislation-teaching-racism/

Toussaint-Strauss, J. (2020, November 26). *How 'voodoo' became a metaphor for evil* [Video]. *YouTube*. https://www.youtube.com/watch?v=4amMTitO714

Trouillot, M. (2015). *Silencing the past: Power and the production of history*. Beacon Press.

Waters, T. (2022, April 26). *Wells Fargo Bank sued for race discrimination in mortgage lending practices*. USA Today. https://www.usatoday.com/story/money/2022/04/26/wells-fargo-being-sued-discriminating-against-black-borrowers/7451521001/

Zoboi, I. (2021). Haitian sensation. In S. J. Fennell (Ed.), *Wild tongues can't be tamed: 15 voices from the Latinx Diaspora* (pp. 89–97). Flatiron Books.

Literature Cited

Thomas, A. (2017). *The hate U give*. Balzer + Bray.

Thomas, A. (2021). *Concrete rose*. Balzer + Bray.

Neri, G. (2010). *Yummy: The last days of a Southside shorty* (R. DuBurke, Illus.). Lee & Low.

Zoboi, I. (2017). *American street*. Balzer + Bray.

6

What Could Critical Literacy Pedagogy Look Like in Grade 11?

According to professor and researcher Allan Luke (2012), the educational antecedents to current understandings of critical literacy pedagogy (CLP) focused on "the possibilities of literacy for the critical analysis of self/other relations and the restoration of power to readers" (p. 7). Luke explains that Louise Rosenblatt's (1978) reader response theory pushed back against New Criticism, which emphasized narrow, close readings of texts. In secondary schooling, New Criticism encouraged teachers to view texts as having only one meaning that the teacher interpreted and passed on to students (Morrell, 2008). Obviously, such a perspective does not allow students much interpretative power in the classroom. As Luke explains, though, Rosenblatt's reader response theory emphasized students' personal interpretations of the texts they studied in school, and this approach gave students more power. A critical literacy perspective views the students' and teacher's interpretations of literature as valuable.

CLP invites students to critique the world as it is portrayed in literary texts (Luke, 2012). An excellent way for teachers to engage their students in critical literacy is to teach them different critical literary theories like feminism, Marxism, postcolonial theory, and gender and queer theories (see Appleman, 2015; Burke, 2013). A literary theory is a set of "assumptions" that guide a person's interpretation of literature (Bressler, 2007, p. 8). Using a particular literary theory to interpret literature is like viewing the text through a specific lens that affects how a reader sees each page. Teaching different theories and how to use them to analyze pieces of literature helps students form their own interpretations of texts studied in school, which gives students more power in the classroom. Helping students analyze works from various literary perspectives invites students to consider different interpretive possibilities of texts, which is a valued literacy practice in English language arts (ELA) and something college English professors expect their students to be able to do (Rainey, 2017). The suggested unit outlined in this chapter aims to support students in gaining access to valued literacy practices like producing a literary analysis using a critical literary theory, but it also aims to support students in speaking to, speaking back to, and speaking against power and injustice. First, though, I will discuss how the literary works often studied in grade 11 offer a multitude of opportunities for critical literacy and for teaching for CHANGE.

Opportunities for Critical Literacy Pedagogy with Grade 11 Curriculum

Most ELA curricula for grade 11 emphasize the study of American literature. Often, the texts that receive the most attention, like F. Scott Fitzgerald's *The Great Gatsby* and John Steinbeck's *Of Mice and Men*, were written by White men. An immediate opportunity for CLP, therefore, presents itself: Teachers can challenge the traditional canon and devote more attention to texts written by people of color and women. Many teachers likely already do this with shorter texts, like poems, short stories, and speeches. When I taught grade 11 ELA, my students and I studied an excerpt of N. Scott Momaday's memoir *The Way to Rainy Mountain* as well as other shorter texts by Native Americans. We also read the short stories "The Yellow Wallpaper" by Charlotte Perkins Gilman and "The Story of an Hour" by Kate Chopin to introduce students to early American feminist perspectives. I taught poetry by Langston Hughes, short stories by Alice Walker, and essays by James Baldwin to try to highlight Black voices. Like I did, many teachers may, for example, connect the works of Henry David Thoreau with those of Dr. Martin Luther King, Jr. or Mohandas Gandhi. Challenging the traditional White canon by diversifying it with shorter texts is important, but studying a novel takes time. When teachers devote more time in their curricula to texts written by White men, they may unintentionally convey the message to students that those works are more important than ones written by people of color and women, which maintains traditional White voices "as the singularity of truth and authority" (Aquino & Khodos, 2020, p. 213).

To communicate a different message to students, educators Kate Aquino and Gena Khodos (2020) decided to "revolutionize" the American literary canon they taught students in suburban Chicago. They designed their revolutionized curriculum to focus on previously overlooked "revolutions and revolutionaries of today" (p. 214). Using Angie Thomas's young adult novel *The Hate U Give* as an anchor text, Aquino and Khodos invited their students to explore topics that connected to the novel, like double-consciousness, the Black Panthers, Tupac Shakur's activism, police brutality, implicit bias and White privilege, and the Black Lives Matter movements by reading additional texts written by people of color.

Aquino and Khodos wanted their students to realize that these were not just supplementary texts and topics "to be told alongside the American Revolution; [they were part] of the story of an American revolution" (p. 219). Aquino and Khodos pointed out that, sadly, while some students responded quite positively to this redesigned curriculum, several did not, and these teachers were accused of "fanning the flames of divisiveness and highlighting the differences of people rather than celebrating" them (p. 222). While they did not use this term in their chapter, I imagine Aquino and Khodos wobbled quite a bit when facing such pushback. By focusing on their values and the importance of a revolutionized curriculum, though, they managed to sustain themselves through their wobbles. They concluded,

> In subverting the traditional canon to present the works of [people of color] as voices of authority in American literature…we show our students the reality we know of this country: Whiteness is not and should not be held up as the standard.
>
> (p. 223)

I agree with them that the voices of people of color and women can no longer be silenced in grade 11 curricula, and the suggested unit presented later in this chapter encourages teachers to replace the study of *Of Mice and Men* with Helena María Viramontes's (1996) novel *Under the Feet of Jesus* (*UTFJ*) to emphasize the voice of a Chicana author and to highlight the experiences of Latinx migrant workers in a racist, exploitative system that continues to this day. You may be able to acquire funds to purchase a class set of *UTFJ* from DonorsChoose (DonorsChoose, n.d.).

Of course, not all teachers will have the option to replace a novel firmly established in the American literary canon. Many teachers are required to teach specific texts, or they are limited to the books available in the English book room. Therefore, before I explain the suggested unit on *UTFJ*, I'll provide suggestions for teaching *The Great Gatsby* and *Of Mice and Men* to promote critical literacy. These novels both invite readers to challenge the concept of "American Dream" and to question for whom it is obtainable, if at all. Both texts offer interpretative possibilities that invite readers to study them using different critical literary theory perspectives to speak back to the abuse of power. In this section, I will provide very brief overviews of some critical literary theories and how they can be applied to *The Great* Gatsby and *Of Mice and Men*. If you plan to teach either of these novels, I recommend that you focus your instruction on speaking against the abuse of power—pointing out abuses of power in the novel is not enough. Students need to have opportunities to speak against such abuses. They can question their own beliefs about justice and the "American Dream," they can create projects and presentations they share with the public, and they can contact legislators with their thoughts on key issues. I'm sure you and your students can come up with other ideas, but the important thing is that students need to do *something* to speak back to power as they study these novels. Later in this section, I provide some suggestions for using these novels to teach for CHANGE.

Teachers can immerse students in critical study of *The Great Gatsby* through feminist, Marxist, and queer theory literary lenses. There is no singular feminist theory, of course, but most approaches to a feminist critique start with the belief that society and culture are "fundamentally patriarchal" and that "all aspects" of culture, including literature, reflect a patriarchal perspective that "marginalizes women and their work" (Dobie, 2009, p. 104). Feminists aim toward revisioning the world to make it more just. Bressler (2007) recommends that, to begin a feminist literary critique of a text, students ask questions like "What types of roles do women have in the text?", "Are the female characters the protagonists or secondary and minor characters?", "What are the attitudes toward women held by the male characters?", and "What is the author's attitude toward women in society?" (p. 184).

You can engage your students in critical literacy by supporting them in analyzing the women characters in *The Great Gatsby*. Jordan's character could be examined to see the attitudes the men characters hold toward the women characters. Nick is fascinated by Jordan's body and behavior, but she is a liar, which smacks of misogyny, and Tom, a staunch defender of a racist patriarchy, believes Jordan's family should not let her be as independent as she is. Students could also examine Daisy's character, for from the very first chapter, Daisy is described as a beautiful and enchanting person who is dissatisfied and untrustworthy. Daisy's comment upon the birth of her daughter, that she hoped she would be attractive but ignorant, can be analyzed to investigate how women were treated leading up to and during the 1920s. Myrtle and her friends are described judgmentally by Nick, though he seems to enjoy partying with them, and his criticisms of them may be because Myrtle is a woman *and* because she belongs to a different social class from Nick, Daisy, and Tom.

A Marxist reading of a text involves examining class conflicts between the bourgeoisie (i.e., the dominant or ruling social class) and the proletariat (i.e., the "working class"; Bressler, 2007, p. 194). Myrtle, her husband George, Myrtle's friends, and the great Gatsby himself could all be seen as representing the proletariat in the novel, while Tom and Daisy, even more than Nick, represent the bourgeoisie. From a Marxist perspective, in a capitalist system, "the rich become richer, and the poor become poorer and increasingly more oppressed" as the ruling class's "ideas, customs, and practices" become the dominant ones forced upon the proletariat (Bressler, p. 194). Dobie (2009) provides some questions to guide a Marxist reading of texts: Readers can ask questions like "Who are the powerless people?", "Why do the powerful people have their power?", and "Why is this power denied to others?" (p. 91). Bressler (2007) includes questions to guide literary analysis through a Marxist lens: "Which characters are oppressed, and to what social classes do they belong?", "Which characters are the oppressors?", and "Is the narrator a member of the bourgeoisie or the proletariat?" (p. 205).

If you have taught *The Great Gatsby* before, you already know the many ways this novel can be analyzed through a Marxist lens. The valley of ashes comes immediately to mind, as do the characters who live and work there. The way Fitzgerald describes George Wilson seemingly disappearing into the bleak background communicates that George is insignificant. Tom certainly views George that way. When I taught this novel, I always emphasized this stark contrast and how many unnamed characters live and toil in the valley of ashes so that people like Tom, Daisy, Gatsby, Nick, and Jordan can party and celebrate a beautiful life away from the pollution caused by their partying. Of course, the bourgeoisie are not described in glowing terms, for Nick criticizes them more than he does the proletariat. Paying attention to how Nick describes Tom, Daisy, and Jordan, from a Marxist perspective, helps the reader understand Fitzgerald's ironic critique of the bourgeoisie of his day.

When I taught *The Great Gatsby*, I always emphasized Nick's commentary after George kills Gatsby in which Nick points out the acute selfishness of Tom and Daisy. Tom and Daisy destroyed people's lives so they could carry on enjoying theirs. Teachers interested in extending a Marxist reading of the novel could support students in investigating current examples of how people experiencing poverty are sacrificed across the globe so the richest few can carry on living lavish lifestyles (e.g., fast fashion, the exportation of U.S. recyclable materials to other countries to process, and the mining of metals and materials for electronic vehicles, cell phones, and other technological devices).

In my dissertation research, Mrs. Skipmann helped students read *The Great Gatsby* through feminist and Marxist lenses. She did not feel supported enough by the school district, though, to engage the whole class in reading the novel using a queer lens. Some of her students who identified as queer[1] read the novel this way on their own, but in the politically conservative state where my study took place, many legislators, administrators, parents and guardians, students, and even teachers were opposed to queer theory. Many believed that LGBTQIA+ perspectives should not be discussed in class, and there were calls by the public for the school district to ban books featuring LGBTQIA+ characters from classrooms. I am not trying to judge Mrs. Skipmann, for she realized that teaching queer theory was not something she was able to do when I observed her teaching, because the idea of doing so caused her too much wobble at the time. Each teacher experiences wobble differently and for different reasons. Mrs. Skipmann did not feel supported enough to try to introduce students to queer theory, and if anyone should be blamed, it is the school district and state legislators across the country who did not rise to defend teachers when they and their profession were "under attack" by the censorship of classroom discourse and book bans (see Hines & Penn, 2023, p. 17).

The Great Gatsby, though, is practically begging to be analyzed through a queer lens. Queer theory is sometimes viewed as emerging from a dissatisfaction with feminist theory's "exclusion of gay women" (Dobie, 2009, p. 111). Queer theorists maintain that "sexuality is neither stable nor static" but is "dynamic and changing, affected by the experience of race and class and subject to shifting desire" (Dobie, 2009, p. 113), and a queer lens demands that readers reject heterosexuality as the "norm against which other sexual identities are measured" (Dobie, p. 113). Dobie provides questions that can guide a queer reading: "Does the work challenge traditional ways of viewing sexuality and identity?", "What sexual topics do you find in the work that are odd or peculiar–that is, queer?", and "Does the work show how sexual identities are indeterminate, overlapping, changing? If so, where?" (pp. 113–114). Bressler (2007) also offers guiding questions to begin a queer reading of a text: "What does it mean to be heterosexual? Homosexual? Gay? Lesbian? Bisexual? Queer?", "What does it mean to be masculine? Feminine?", and "What is a 'macho' man?" (p. 255).

You can help students ask questions like these while studying *The Great Gatsby*. Though Tom's sexuality is not really a question in the novel, students could still engage in a queer reading of his character by examining this question "What is a 'macho' man?" Tom's muscles and physical mass are frequently described by Nick. He was a star athlete and had at least two sexual affairs after marrying Daisy. Tom is strong, confident, rich, and domineering, and he is an abuser. Tom is also deeply disappointed with his life, despite his wealth and accomplishments. What does his character have to say about toxic masculinity and what it means to be "macho"?

More interesting than Tom, of course, is Nick. For example, students might ask "What sexual topics do you find in the work that are odd or peculiar—that is, queer?" while reading the end of Chapter 2 when Nick ends up in a state of undress with Mr. McKee in bed and drunkenly looking at photographs. Asking this question could prompt a very interesting class discussion of Nick's indeterminate sexuality. Nick has romantic relationships with women, including one back home that he realizes needs to end because he enjoys kissing Jordan, but this scene with Mr. McKee also portrays Nick as someone who is potentially open to other sexual experiences. His relationship with the woman back home further encourages discussion of the questions of "What does it mean to be masculine? Feminine?" because Nick mentions the woman he was dating back home gets a mustache of sweat when she plays tennis that bothers him. It seems Nick does not want his partner to look too traditionally masculine, yet when Nick mentions enjoying looking at Jordan's body, he emphasizes that she threw her body backward like a soldier, which would be considered more masculine at the time. Obviously, Nick is fascinated by Gatsby so much that readers must wonder about Nick's sexuality—just look at the way Nick describes Gatsby's smile. Reading the novel through a queer lens creates exciting interpretative possibilities for students.

Reading Steinbeck's *Of Mice and Men* through feminist and Marxists lenses also affords students exciting interpretative possibilities. In *Of Mice and Men*, apart from Lennie's Aunt Clara being briefly mentioned, only one woman character is present, and the reader never learns her name. She is usually referred to as Curley's wife, but the men on the ranch also call her sexist names. Teachers can encourage students to analyze her character through a feminist lens by asking some of the questions recommended by Bressler (2007): "What types of roles do women have in the text?", "Are the female characters the protagonists or secondary and minor characters?", and "What are the attitudes toward women held by the male characters?" (p. 184). Curley's wife is a secondary character who nevertheless contributes greatly to the novel's rising action and climax. She remains a nameless character but her body is described in great detail. Students could investigate what her life is like being married to a miserable man like Curley and being kept from pursuing her dreams in the movie industry. Steinbeck perhaps intended to leave her unnamed to further illustrate the way the men characters view her, as a beautiful body not worth speaking to or even as dangerous because of her sexual advances. You can help students analyze the misogynistic ways she is discussed by the men characters, who should be able to empathize with her loneliness but do not. To engage students further in critical literacy, you could facilitate discussions of how women who express sensuality are treated in the media and society today.

It is almost impossible to study *Of Mice and Men* without engaging in a Marxist reading, for Steinbeck was not particularly subtle in his critique of capitalism in his novels. Obviously, characters like the Boss and Curley are the oppressors, and they have the power to oppress because they own the land the characters work. George, Lennie, and the other migrant ranch workers are the proletariat being oppressed by the Boss. In the novel, the need for work (and the little pay the workers receive) is a constant pressure on George and Lennie.

Because they have no one else to look after them, they must look after each other and earn as much money as they can before Lennie inevitably gets the pair in trouble and they have to move to another ranch, owned by some other nameless Boss. Their dream is to save enough money to buy their own ranch. A Marxist reading of this novel would investigate how the workers are mistreated by the Boss and his son. Students could investigate Steinbeck's theme regarding the "American Dream" and if it is attainable at all for the characters, whose 11-hour days working land for someone else's financial gain are sure to continue after the conclusion of the novel. To further engage in critical literacy, students could investigate the "American Dream" today and could examine ways that workers continue to be oppressed across the globe. You could facilitate class discussions on issues regarding minimum wage, migrant workers' pay, and student loan debt, for example.

To use these novels to teach for CHANGE, you may want to pursue some of these suggestions:

- ♦ Using online tools, your students could survey their peers at your school regarding their perspectives of women. You and your students could brainstorm questions to be included in the survey and then analyze the results to interrogate misogyny present in their peers' views. Depending on the results, you may ask students to create a presentation to share with their classmates virtually or at a school assembly to address concerns you and your students identified from the results.
- ♦ Your students could investigate statistics about average earnings in your state or city to explore questions inspired by a Marxist reading of the novels. Additionally, students could analyze social media to interrogate what "ruling ideas" are influencing them and their generation. They could write reflective pieces exploring how they feel about the messages they consume daily regarding wealth and the "American Dream."
- ♦ After interpreting *The Great Gatsby* using a queer lens, you and your students may decide to start a Genders and Sexualities Alliance (GSA; GSA Network, n.d.) club if your school does not have one already. If it does, you and your students can find ways to support the club's efforts.

In addition to these suggestions, I recommend that you, your students, and your colleagues work together to brainstorm even better ways to use these novels to teach for CHANGE.

Finally, I'd like to discuss two points about using *The Great Gatsby* and *Of Mice and Men* to provide CLP. First, these novels do allow teachers and students to discuss issues surrounding race and racism, and many teachers try to use these texts by White men to do exactly that. In *The Great Gatsby*, for example, Tom's White supremacist views are on display in the very first chapter. In *Of Mice and Men*, the only Black character, Crooks, is discriminated against by almost every other character. When my students and I studied the novel, I instructed them not read the racial slurs used for Crooks out loud (but they see the words in the text, so the potential for harm is great), and we discussed the racist actions by characters in the novel. Many teachers likely help students recognize the racism in these novels, and like I used to do, they may tell students that both Fitzgerald and Steinbeck included racism in their fiction to challenge the real racism of their day. Recently, I've spoken with a secondary ELA teacher who teaches American literature. Through our conversations, they have helped me see that Fitzgerald and Steinbeck can—at the same time—criticize racism in their works while advancing racist views. As this teacher helped me realize, an author can simultaneously criticize something and perpetuate it. Yes, teachers can use these novels as tools to challenge racism, but they are not the best tools to use to accomplish that goal.

The second point I want to emphasize about using these novels for CLP is that while these texts can be used to perform feminist literary analysis, other texts written by women are better options for highlighting feminist perspectives. Also, when supporting students in engaging in feminist readings of these novels, teachers may want to highlight the ways that American feminism has, at times, excluded women of color (see Crenshaw, 1991; hooks, 1994) in addition to how it initially excluded queer and lesbian women (Dobie, 2009). While these novels have great potential for supporting students in critical literacy, I believe there are other novels that address issues of genders and sexualities, race and racism, and the exploitation of workers and that should be included in a critically redesigned grade 11 ELA curriculum.

If you have the autonomy and the funding, I suggest you replace the study of *Of Mice and Men* with Helena María Viramontes's (1996) novel *UTFJ* to immerse students in Challenging injustice to Help make a difference by Asking and answering tough questions and Noticing ways to Get involved and Engaged in making the world more just.

Overview of the Environmental Justice Unit for CHANGE

This unit gets students to read and analyze *UTFJ* to perform an ecofeminist, environmental justice, and Marxist interpretation of the text, resulting in activism of some sort. The unit involves students in critical analysis to address this question: How are some of the injustices in the novel still happening today, and what can we do about it? Critical scholar Paulo Freire (1970/2018) argued that critical literacy should result in praxis (i.e., "reflection and action upon the world in order to transform it"; p. 51). If you decide to teach this unit, the critical reading of *UTFJ* should end up giving your students opportunities to do something about the injustices and abuses of power they discuss while studying the novel.

Viramontes dedicated *UTFJ* to Cesar Chavez. Chavez was inspired by Dr. King and Gandhi, and along with his family, Dolores Huerta, and other community organizers, he formed the United Farm Workers organization which uses nonviolence as a tool to advocate for agricultural workers' rights and well-being (United Farm Workers, n.d.). Using tactics like boycotting grapes, workers' strikes, and fasting, Chavez and the United Farm Workers' actions resulted in improved conditions for agricultural laborers in California (Kirk, 1998). The United Farm Workers (n.d.) webpage has tabs with information and opportunities to "Take Action" and get involved in "Creating Change," and I suggest you work with your students to participate in some kind of activism or action after reading the novel. You and your students may decide to send letters to legislators and government administrators regarding the use of pesticides, to boycott a particular produce product, to support a farmer's market, or to create a school food pantry or garden. You know your school context and local possibilities for activism better than I do, but if you decide to teach this unit, please brainstorm with your colleagues and students so that the unit results in praxis so you and your students can advocate for needed CHANGE.

Viramontes's *UTFJ* takes place in California's Central Valley where the main characters, who are Mexican-American migrant agricultural workers, labor in the fields and orchards. The story follows Estrella, who is entering her teenage years. Estrella is the oldest child of her mother Petra and absent father. At the beginning of the novel, Estrella, her mother, her younger siblings, and Perfecto, a man in his seventies who is romantically involved with Petra, arrive at a new farm looking for work. This is similar to the beginning of Steinbeck's *Of Mice and Men*, and just like George and Lennie, Estrella and her family think constantly of work.

In addition to the family's struggles to secure work and make their money last, the novel focuses on Estrella's coming of age as a young woman who discovers her critical consciousness. Her critical consciousness is awakened when another teenager working the fields, Alejo (who is romantically interested in Estrella), is poisoned by pesticides sprayed directly on him when the owners of the fields had them sprayed ahead of schedule. Alejo becomes so sick that Estrella persuades Petra and Perfecto to take him to a clinic. After talking with a seemingly uncaring nurse, Estrella realizes that she, her family, and Alejo will not receive the attention and care they deserve, and she realizes that she and other racialized and marginalized agricultural laborers are sacrificed so that the privileged and wealthy can continue enjoying their lives in their air-conditioned cars, removed from the dangerous, bone-dissolving work of the fields. Because developing sociopolitical consciousness is a key concept of critical thought (Dyches, 2018), this novel is an excellent tool to support students in practicing critical literacy. This novel, just like *The Great Gatsby* and *Of Mice and Men*, forces readers to question the "American Dream" and to challenge the economic system of the United States that exploits many for the benefit of the relative few. Just like those novels, *UTFJ* uses powerful metaphors (e.g., a statue of Jesus) and striking imagery to convey Viramontes's themes relating to the abuses of power and injustices rampant in U.S. agribusiness (see Corchado, 2020; Jordan, 2023; Moses, 1993).

The Environmental Justice Unit Lesson Plans

Because studying the novel through ecofeminist and environmental justice lenses requires students to be familiar with Marxist literary theory, I suggest that you teach *UTFJ* after your students have studied *The Great Gatsby*. The following lesson plans focus mostly on critical aspects of the unit, not everything you would need to do to support students in a rigorous study of the novel.

The Environmental Justice Unit Lesson Plan 1

When to implement this lesson:	After students have read Part 1
Lesson objective:	Students will apply tenets of ecofeminism and environmental justice movements to perform a critical reading of the first part of the novel.
Assessment:	Students will take notes on ecofeminism and environmental justice movements and will begin analyzing the novel through those lenses. Students will participate in a class discussion.
Suggested texts needed:	A teacher-made handout summarizing notes on some ecofeminist and environmental justice tenets and approaches to literary analysis
Suggested activities:	♦ Provide students with notes on ecofeminist and environmental justice approaches to analyzing literature. You can use the following points: ○ Ecofeminism in the United States started in the 1970s, following women's liberation movements, when Susan Griffin and Carolyn Merchant began to explore "the connection between the domination of women and the domination of nature, where nature is often feminized and sexualized as in 'virgin forest,' 'the rape of the earth,' or 'penetrating' the wilderness" (Kirk, 1998, pp. 177–178). ○ Ecofeminist literary theory points out that "where to place nuclear waste dumps" and other environmental problems "is both an ecological and a feminist task because the uses and abuses of the environment that have led to what they see as the potentially catastrophic present are largely due to a patriarchal environmental ethic that has conceptualized land as 'woman'" (Legler, 1997, pp. 227–228). ○ One question that guides an ecofeminist reading is "How can developing an ecocritical literary theory help solve real environmental problems?" (Legler, 1997, p. 228).

(Continued)

	<ul><li>For interpreting *UTFJ*, I suggest that students ask, "How does the treatment of the main characters in this novel relate to the ways humans treat nature?"</li><li>One thing early ecofeminist theories seemed to ignore was that "patriarchal capitalist systems also involve exploitation based on race and class" in addition to gender (Kirk, 1998, p. 178).</li><li>Kirk suggests that ecofeminist theories can help environmental justice movements gain "an understanding of how the domination of nature is linked to the domination of women, and how sexism is a key mechanism of oppression with parallels to racial and class oppression" (p. 193).</li><li>Environmental justice movements that emphasize the concerns of Chicanx people, who "see environmental issues in the wider context of race, class, and cultural oppression" (Kirk, 1998, p. 188), address "the struggle for economic and environmental justice" and "a demand for healthful living and working conditions" (Kirk, p. 182).</li><li>Since the 1990s, there has been a shift of emphasis from preserving nature "as a good in itself" to an emphasis of "social justice" (Buell, 2001, p. 33).</li><li>This shift resulted in the concept of environmental racism, which is "racial discrimination in environmental policymaking" (Chavis, 1993, p. 3). Examples of environmental racism are "problems of lead, pesticides, and petrochemical plants that have a disproportionately large impact on communities of color" (p. 4).</li></ul><ul><li>Once students have taken notes on these approaches to analyzing literature, ask them to spend time discussing with a partner how what they've just learned connects to *UTFJ*. Require the partners to record key scenes and quotes from the novel that connect to ecofeminism and environmental justice.</li><li>Then facilitate a class discussion on the interpretative possibilities of reading the novel through ecofeminist and environmental justice lenses. Even though I know you know how to lead class discussions, I like to share my suggestions in case you find them helpful:<ul><li>Remind students of class rules and norms.</li><li>Print out example sentence starters and tape them to each student's desk so they can practice using the discourse valued in respectful discussions. For example, I might use some sentence starters they can use to participate in scholarly discourse. To help students state their opinion and defend it with evidence, they could use this sentence starter:</li></ul></li></ul>

(Continued)

	"The author suggests [blank.] Notice what they wrote on page [blank]." To help students disagree respectfully, they could use this sentence starter: "That is one perspective, but I have a different one. What if we view it this way: [blank]?" To keep the discussion going, students could use this sentence starter: "What other perspectives are there, or who has something to say but has not been able to yet?" o If time allows, have students reflect on their participation in the concluded discussion by answering questions like "How did I contribute to the class discussion? Did I contribute mostly by being a good listener, or did I contribute verbally or virtually to the discussion?" and "What would I do differently the next time we have a discussion?"

The Environmental Justice Unit Lesson Plan 2

When to implement this lesson:	After students have read Part 2
Lesson objective:	Students will read a chapter from Rachel Carson's (1962/2002) book *Silent Spring*, which helped start the environmental movement, to analyze her main argument and continue interpreting *UTFJ* through ecofeminist and environmental justice lenses.
Assessment:	Students will annotate an informational text, and they will use their annotations to participate in a class discussion.
Suggested text needed:	Chapter 2 of *Silent Spring*, "The Obligation to Endure"
Suggested activities:	♦ Have students read this short chapter on their own first and tell them their purpose is to discover what they believe Carson's main argument is. ♦ After a brief whole-class discussion of Carson's main argument, have students reread the chapter with a partner or small group. Tell them, this time, their purpose is to read to discover how Carson makes and supports her argument: In addition to ethical, logical, and emotional appeals, Carson uses rhetorical questions, statistics, and strong diction to argue against the abuse of pesticides. ♦ Facilitate a class discussion on Carson's chapter and how it connects to the characters in *UTFJ*.

The Environmental Justice Unit Lesson Plan 3

When to implement this lesson:	Immediately after Lesson Plan 2
Lesson objectives:	Students will read a Cesar Chavez speech to analyze his main points, understand his definition of *nonviolence*, and make connections to the novel to continue studying it through ecofeminist and environmental justice lenses.
Assessment:	Students will read and annotate the speech in small groups, taking notes on the evidence they collect. They will use their notes to participate in a class discussion.
Suggested text needed:	♦ Chavez's speech, "Perils of Pesticides Address to Pacific Lutheran University," which can be accessed online through the Cesar Chavez Foundation (n.d.) website (the link is in the references at the end of this chapter)
Suggested activities:	♦ Begin class by reviewing key tenets of ecofeminist and environmental justice literary theories as well as the class discussion from Lesson Plan 2. ♦ Place students into small groups. Assign each group a different purpose for reading Chavez's speech: (1) Read and annotate the speech to gather evidence that someone concerned about environmental justice and environmental racism might use from this speech. Connect this speech to the novel. (2) Read and annotate the speech to gather evidence that someone performing an ecofeminist reading of the novel might use from this speech. (3) Read and annotate the speech to gather evidence that someone performing a Marxist reading of the novel might use from this speech. ♦ Give students time to read and discuss the speech in their small groups. ♦ Then engage students in a whole-class discussion of Chavez's main points and how they connect to the novel and *Silent Spring*.

The Environmental Justice Unit Lesson Plan 4

When to implement this lesson:	After students have read Part 3
Lesson objectives:	Students will review the novel and reread key scenes to gather evidence of injustices and abuses of power impacting the characters. This lesson introduces students to the critical inquiry question guiding the unit: How are some of the injustices in the novel still happening today, and what can we do about it?
Assessment:	Students will take notes of key abuses of power and moments of injustice they've encountered in the novel.
Suggested texts needed:	No additional texts needed
Suggested activities:	♦ If you have not already, share the guiding critical question to the class: How are some of the injustices in the novel still happening today, and what can we do about it? ♦ Place students in small groups or with a partner and require them to revisit key scenes in the novel and to take notes on the abuses of power and injustices the characters face. I suggest that students take notes in double-entry journals, where on the left side of their notebook paper they write a quote or detail from the novel and on the right side they write a personal response related to the quote/detail (see AdLit, n.d.). ♦ Provide students with passages to reread. Here are some suggested key passages you might want students to discuss: 　o The first two pages describing how much the main characters work 　o Scenes with Maxine (pages 28–38) 　o The foreshadowing of the dangers of pesticides (page 42) 　o The beginning of Part 2 (pages 49–56) that describes the dehumanizing work that Estrella does in the grape fields, child labor, and Alejo's "American Dream" 　o Page 63: When Petra reminds Estrella of the citizenship papers under the feet of Jesus and discusses immigration officers 　o Pages 73–78: When the pesticides are sprayed ahead of schedule and Alejo is poisoned 　o Pages 78–83: When Perfecto fixates on earning enough money to return home 　o Pages 109–110: When Petra is purchasing goods and the only produce available for the laborers to buy are the damaged or bruised items (p. 110)

(Continued)

| | o Page 117: When Alejo and Estrella discuss their dreams
o Page 125: When the pregnant Petra fears what the pesticides might do to the fetus
o Pages 127–130: When their car gets stuck in the mud as Estralla, her family, and Perfecto try to take Alejo to a medical clinic
♦ Facilitate a class discussion on the abuses of power and injustices in the novel. |

The Environmental Justice Unit Lesson Plan 5

When to implement this lesson:	Soon after Lesson Plan 4
Lesson objective:	Students will read and discuss two articles about the experiences of (im)migrant farmworkers in the United States to address the guiding critical question: How are some of the injustices in the novel still happening today, and what can we do about it?
Assessment:	Students will review their notes from Lesson Plan 4 and take notes on the articles. They will use their notes to participate in a class discussion. They will also add to their double-entry journals.
Suggested texts needed:	♦ Alfredo Corchado's (2020) opinion piece titled "A Former Farmworker on American Hypocrisy," published by the *New York Times* ♦ Miriam Jordan's (2023) article titled "Retirement Without a Net: The Plight of America's Aging Farmworkers," published by the *New York Times* The links to these articles are in the references at the end of this chapter.
Suggested activities:	♦ Remind students of the guiding critical question and tell them that as they read this lesson's assigned texts, they should look for information they can use to address the question. ♦ Read the articles with the class and discuss the injustices and abuses of power and make connections to the novel. You and your students might discuss how immigration officers can deport people who are working in U.S. legally if they do not have their papers with them in the fields. ♦ Ask students to add to their double-entry journals during the discussion.

The Environmental Justice Unit Lesson Plan 6

When to implement this lesson:	Soon after Lesson 5
Lesson objectives:	Students will read an article about women's experiences working as farm laborers to make connections to the novel, address the guiding critical inquiry question, and participate in a class discussion.
Assessment:	Students will take notes on the article and use those notes to participate in a class discussion. Students will also add to their double-entry journals.
Suggested texts needed:	Dakin and Moyles's (2016) article titled "Farmworkers push back against machismo and abuse in California's wine country," published by The World by PRX. The link is in the references at the end of this chapter.
Suggested activities:	♦ Assign the article and tell students their purpose is to read it closely to understand women's experiences working in the fields and to address the guiding critical inquiry question. Require students to take notes as they read in their double-entry journals to guide their participation in the discussion. ♦ Facilitate the class discussion and ask students to continue adding to their double-entry journals.

The Environmental Justice Unit Lesson Plan 7

When to implement this lesson:	After students have read Part 4
Lesson objectives:	♦ Students will reread and discuss a key scene in the novel in which Estrella becomes critically aware of the abuses of power around her. ♦ Students will write a personal essay about a time when they became aware of an injustice in the world.
Assessment:	Students will turn in their personal essays.
Suggested texts needed:	No additional texts needed
Suggested activities:	♦ Review Part 4 as needed, and you will need to review Alejo and Estrella's conversation about tar pits (see pages 85–89). ♦ Tell students that an important concept of critical theory is consciousness-raising (Morrell, 2008) or developing "sociopolitical consciousness," which means becoming aware of the way power works in politics and society and pushing back against the abuse of power (Dyches, 2018, p. 38).

(Continued)

	♦ Ask students to reread pages 143–150 to understand Estrella's moment of critical consciousness. ♦ Discuss with students what Estrella has discovered in these pages. ♦ Then ask students to write a personal essay about a time when they became sociopolitically or critically aware of an injustice in the world and to reflect on that important moment in their lives.

The Environmental Justice Unit Lesson Plan 8

When to implement this lesson:	Immediately after students have had time to write, revise, and share the essays they started in Lesson Plan 7
Lesson objectives:	Students will read three articles about a pesticide recently banned in the U.S. to make connections to the novel, address the guiding critical inquiry question, and participate in a class discussion.
Assessment:	Students will annotate and take notes on the articles. They will use their notes to participate in a class discussion.
Suggested texts needed:	♦ Romo's (2021) article titled "EPA will ban a farming pesticide linked to health problems in children" ♦ Charles's (2021) article titled "Toxic pesticide faces new scrutiny from Biden administration" ♦ Gonzalez's (2019) article titled "California bans popular pesticide linked to brain damage in children" These articles are all published by NPR, and the links are available in the references at the end of this chapter.
Suggested activities:	♦ Start the lesson by reminding students of Carson's point in *Silent Spring* that the public has a right to know the facts about pesticide usage in the United States. ♦ Then ask students to read and annotate the three articles. I suggest beginning with Romo's (2021) article. ♦ Facilitate a class discussion of the articles. Ask students to add to their double-entry journals during the discussion.

The Environmental Justice Unit Lesson Plan 9

When to implement this lesson:	After students have finished reading the novel
Lesson objective:	Students will analyze the novel using a critical literary theory (ecofeminist, environmental justice, or Marxist).
Assessment:	Students will write a literary analysis of the novel.
Suggested texts needed:	I do not suggest that students read these articles, but they were helpful for me when designing this unit, so you may want to read them yourself: ♦ "'The oil was made from their bones': Environmental (in)justice in Helena María Viramontes's *Under the Feet of Jesus*" by Grewe-Volpp (2005) ♦ "'You talk 'merican?': Class, value, and the social production of difference in Helena María Viramontes's *Under the Feet of Jesus*" by López (2014)
Suggested activities:	♦ Ask students to decide which theory they would like to use to analyze the novel. Place students in small groups according to their selected theories. ♦ Instruct the groups to review their double-entry journals as well as key scenes from the novel to identify what they should analyze and how their selected lens will influence their analysis. ♦ Give groups time to find excerpts of the novel to use in their literary analysis essays and to brainstorm. ♦ Then support students as needed in composing and revising their literary analysis essays.

The Environmental Justice Unit Lesson Plan 10

When to implement this lesson:	After students have completed their literary analysis essays of *UTFJ*
Lesson objectives:	Students will conduct research on ways that youth can engage in activism and will plan what you all as a class will do to address current injustices that echo those present in the novel.
Assessment:	Students will select and plan a way to engage in effective activism.
Suggested texts needed:	The online article titled "10 Ways Youth Can Engage in Activism," published by the Anti-Defamation League (2017). The link is in the references at the end of this chapter.

(Continued)

Suggested activities:	♦ Review and discuss the critical inquiry question: How are some of the injustices in the novel still happening today, and what can we do about it? ♦ Ask students to pick an injustice occurring today that is similar to one in the novel to address as a class. ♦ Support students in researching and brainstorming ways to make a CHANGE based on their study of the novel. ♦ Guide the class in deciding what you can do to advocate for CHANGE. ♦ Together, plan your next steps and begin. Depending on what you and students decide, because of time and curricular demands, you may need to work on advocating for CHANGE as you begin another unit of study.

Anticipated Moments of Wobble with the Environmental Justice Unit

As I created each unit for this book, I've considered what might make me wobble if I taught them. The Environmental Justice Unit causes me the least imagined wobble of all the units. Of course, wobble is a personal experience, so if you experienced a lot of anticipatory wobble while reading over this unit, please don't be discouraged. I do imagine ways this unit could cause wobble. Probably the largest wobble could occur from fear of the accusations that students and parents or guardians might levy against you. It is possible that some would view the goal and activities of this unit as being "anti-American," "anti-Trump," and "pro-communist."

Anticipated Moments of Wobble with Specific Lesson Plans
The first lesson plan may cause wobble as you introduce students to concepts like environmental justice and environmental racism. You may be accused of indoctrinating youth or "teaching Critical Race Theory" (CRT). I can think of two ways to address this wobble: First, remember that sharing the tenets of different critical approaches to studying literature is one of the

many responsibilities of being an ELA teacher (Appleman, 2015). Second, people are less likely to accuse you of indoctrination if you are careful with your word and phrasing choices. If you frame your instruction in this lesson as informing students what these different critics believe—not that your students must agree with these tenets—it is less likely you can be accused of indoctrination. Please see the previous chapter for my suggestions for dealing with accusations that you're "teaching CRT."

You may fear being accused of providing "anti-American" and "pro-communist" instruction for Lesson Plan 3. Thankfully, I feel this wobble can be addressed easily. Please remember that Chavez's speech encourages nonviolence, so even if you were promoting an "anti-American" sentiment, which I don't think you will be, if your solution is nonviolence, who could really object all that much? Also, remember that traditional grade 11 curricula include Thoreau's letter on civil disobedience and often include excerpts of Dr. King or Gandhi's writings. This lesson plan is no more "anti-American" than other lessons on nonviolence often taught in grade 11 curricula.

The fourth lesson introduces students to the guiding critical question about current injustices and encourages students to think of ways to advocate for CHANGE. Some students or their parents and guardians could see this guiding question as imposing an agenda on students. Fear of how students and their parents/guardians may respond could cause wobble for you. I suggest that you sustain yourself through that wobble by focusing on this fact: Advocating for CHANGE as a result of reading *UTFJ* makes the study of American literature more rigorous and relevant to students than simply reading a novel to take a multiple-choice test. Most parents and guardians would agree that schooling should be relevant to their children's lives and should help them be better prepared to engage in the world beyond high school.

I imagine that you might experience some wobble when preparing to teach the fifth and sixth suggested lessons because the articles focus on some injustices impacting (im)migrant farm laborers. Some students and their parents or guardians might charge you with being "anti-Trump" and with supporting people for breaking the law. You may also be afraid that some of your students will repeat harmful rhetoric against people who are immigrants. As I'm sure you do already, anytime you discuss a potentially controversial topic with students, you want to review your norms for class discussions. That can help you address concerns about problematic statements your students might make. Regarding concerns about how parents or guardians might respond to these lessons, please remember that discussing the issues involved with U.S. immigration policies and how that impacts the food that Americans purchase and eat helps make the novel more relevant to their lives. Immigration is an important and relevant topic for your students and the United States as a nation, and students deserve the opportunity to discuss such important topics in class, especially when doing so connects to the literature they are studying.

Some may object to the emphasis on Estrella's awakening to her sociopolitical consciousness in Lesson Plan 7. You may experience wobble if you anticipate some student or parent/guardian pushback against critical theory. Because you will likely experience this kind of wobble again in Lesson Plan 10, I'll further address this below.

Because the articles that students will read in the eighth lesson plan discuss how the Biden administration overruled a Trump administration decision and banned the pesticide chlorpyrifos, some may accuse you of promoting an "anti-Trump" and "pro-Biden" political agenda. As always, when teaching facts to students, emphasizing those facts (and not personally commenting on them) is a great way to address this type of wobble. The Trump administration likely did not ban chlorpyrifos because of a difference between Republican and Democrat views on government regulations. Helping students understand that members of these two political parties have different views on the role of government is not promoting one party over another. So, if you are careful with your word choices and how you respond to student comments, I believe you can teach this lesson without pushing a political agenda.

For Lesson Plans 9 and 10 (and 7), you may experience wobble because these lessons promote critical theory and critical praxis. Some parents and guardians may oppose the idea of activism and accuse you of indoctrinating students and of "making everything political." If I were teaching this unit, I would address this wobble by reminding myself that promoting critical praxis makes the study of this novel more rigorous and relevant to students than traditional ways of teaching novels. As Mrs. Skipmann and Mr. Tophill had to do to sustain themselves through the wobbles they experienced when teaching, all teachers must let their values guide their teaching decisions. If you value rigorous, relevant study that helps students do something inside and outside the classroom that matters to them and helps make the world a better place, you will be able to endure the wobbles this unit causes you. I'm not saying it will be easy, but ultimately, focusing on your values can help you increase your stretchiness for wobble with this unit. Furthermore, Lesson Plan 10 encourages you to work with students to decide together what form your activism will take. This should help you repel accusations that you are indoctrinating students. If you give students agency in the classroom, it is more difficult for their parents or guardians to argue that you imposed something on them.

Encouragement to Expand Your Stretchiness

If you have experienced some anticipatory wobble when considering teaching this unit, I offer suggestions for expanding your stretchiness so you can teach it even though it is causing you to wobble. In general, my suggestions are the same for each recommended unit for grades 9, 10, 11, and 12: (1) collaborate with your English teacher peers, school administrators, and parents and guardians; (2) adjust the unit as necessary; (3) create a rationale you can use to defend your pedagogical decisions; and (4) spend some time reflecting on where your discomfort is coming from and what your wobbles tell you about your teaching practice and your needs as a human and teacher. Below, I make each of these suggestions specific to the Environmental Justice Unit.

Collaborate with Your English Teacher Peers, School Administrators, and Parents/Guardians

Work with the other grade 11 ELA teachers so that together you can adjust the suggested lesson plans as you see fit. For example, if you live in a state far removed from concerns about agribusiness, you all may decide to investigate related issues and injustices, like fast fashion or the use of "forever chemicals." You can also collaborate to create a rationale to defend your pedagogical decisions or revise the recommended letter to parents and guardians I've included in the Appendices (see Appendix D). Your experiences with wobble will likely be easier for you if you collaborate with your peers.

As a team, you can work with your school administrators to help them see the value of this unit for your students (and maybe ask them to purchase copies of *UTFJ* for your department). I believe your administrators can support you if you help them understand what you plan to do in and outside of class. They may even suggest ways that you and your peers have not thought of to get students involved in activism.

Parents and guardians deserve to know what their children are doing in class and deserve to have a chance to support that work and you as the teacher. I suggest that you communicate with parents and guardians honestly and openly—even if that can create some wobble for you. Getting them "on your side" through open communication can reduce your experiences with wobble. If parents and guardians can see the value of this unit, they can support their children in getting the most out of it. To get teens involved in activism requires the collective efforts of students, their parents/guardians, administrators, and, of course, you and the other grade 11 ELA teachers.

Adjust the Unit

As discussed in previous chapters, Garcia and O'Donnell-Allen (2015) compared wobble to practicing yoga, and I like to return to that metaphor when thinking about adjusting the suggested units. If you practice yoga and try out a new pose, you will probably wobble a little bit on the mat or shake because the needed muscles might not be strong enough yet. If you ever want to accomplish the pose, you will need to respond to the wobble by making slight adjustments, which will allow you to practice the pose long enough for the required muscles to develop and for your balance to build—with time and practice. This metaphor applies to the Environmental Justice Unit. If you make needed adjusts to the unit so you can still teach it, you may eventually be able to engage students in critical literacy for CHANGE by doing the Environmental Justice Unit exactly as I've described here—or by teaching your own unit that is better than mine!

You may experience the most anticipatory wobble regarding the unit's call to activism. If that is keeping you from trying to teach the unit, I suggest dropping the activism piece the first time you teach it. Replacing the study of a novel you may have taught for years with a new one is a lot of work. Engaging students in activism is a lot of work too, and if the thought of doing so is causing you too much wobble right now, please still teach this unit. You can promote critical literacy, challenge the traditional American literature canon which silences the voices of people of color and women, and teach for CHANGE. Try this unit once without the activism piece and see if you can expand your stretchiness for wobble so the next time you teach it, you can include the call to activism.

Create a Rationale

If you decide to use the Environmental Justice Unit (even with some slight adjustments), I suggest that you prepare a rationale. First, as it did for Mrs. Skipmann, creating a rationale can help you expand your stretchiness for wobble, which makes it easier to experience and respond to other wobbles in future. Second, preparing a rationale requires you to articulate why you think the unit is valuable, and you can communicate that to your colleagues, administrators, your students, and their parents/guardians. Even parents or guardians who disagree with you will find it difficult to be mean or disrespectful to you if you are able to communicate clearly your passion for teaching the unit and the value you believe your instruction holds for their children. As you think about your rationale, think about your teaching philosophy and what you feel is most important in ELA instruction. Here are some additional points to consider:

- As I wrote in the previous chapter, if you are concerned that teaching this unit will result in accusations that you are "teaching CRT," you can defend yourself by reading and citing the National Council of Teachers of English's (NCTE) position statement titled, "Educators' Right and Responsibilities to Engage in Antiracist Teaching" (NCTE, 2022).
- You may experience wobble because you're concerned about promoting activism and you may fear being accused of imposing a political agenda on students. If you're concerned about that, please remember, no curriculum is neutral: "what counts as legitimate knowledge is the result of complex power relations and struggles among identifiable class, race, gender, and religious groups" (Apple, 1992, p. 4). For decades, American literature curricula have emphasized the works of White men and devalued those written by people of color and women. Were those decisions neutral? A decision not to teach this unit is just as political as the decision to teach it. Also, even traditional American literature curricula engage students in considering political implications of what they read in class. When students read Thoreau and Dr. King, don't they also consider ways to protest injustice and abuses of power through nonviolence? Additionally, the Common Core standards for grade 11 require students to read political documents like *The Declaration of Independence* and the Bill of Rights (National Governors Association Center for Best Practices & Council of Chief State School Officers, 2010; RI.11–12.9). No grade 11 curriculum has ever been politically neutral.
- According to a recent report by the Pew Research Center, 58% of high school teachers stated that "students showing

little or no interest in learning is a major problem in their classroom" (Lin et al., 2024, p. 8). I believe that CLP immerses students in exciting work, and I believe that when teachers engage students in meaningful work, students will show interest in their learning. Therefore, I believe the Environmental Justice Unit can get students interested in what they're studying in class, which can help students learn what they need to be prepared for what is next in their futures. Most parents and guardians would agree that is a goal worth accomplishing.

Using some of the points above, I've written an example letter you could send to parents and guardians (see Appendix D). You are welcome to use the letter, but you will want to include the correct contact information.

Spend Time Reflecting

This concluding section is essentially the same in Chapters 4, 5, 6, and 7 because the advice applies to all experiences of wobble caused from teaching for CHANGE. While I've discussed some moments of wobble I think you might experience if you implement the Environmental Justice Unit, each teacher experiences wobble differently. Moments of wobble often produce feelings of fear. In his book *The Heart of the Buddha's Teaching: Transforming Suffering into Peace, Joy, and Liberation*, the late Buddhist monk and teacher Thich Nhat Hanh discusses the importance of mindfully acknowledging our feelings and letting them run through our minds without judgment. Hanh (2015) wrote, "when our feelings are stronger than our mindfulness, we suffer" (p. 73). If you're wobbling as you consider implementing this unit, that's okay! Your wobble does not have to make you suffer. Take some time to reflect on what your feelings are telling you about your teaching practice and about yourself as a human. Look deeply into them, without judging yourself or allowing the feelings to take over. I hope you'll find that pausing and reflecting will give you perspective and produce wisdom that you can apply to your teaching practice.

Note

1 The word *queer* continues to be used in hurtful ways, but many people use the word "with pride to identify themselves" (Planned Parenthood, n.d., para 2).

References

Anti-Defamation League. (2017, January 17). *10 ways youth can engage in activism*. https://www.adl.org/resources/tools-and-strategies/10-ways-youth-can-engage-activism

Apple, M. W. (1992). The text and cultural politics. *Educational Researcher, 21*(7), 4–11+19.

Appleman, D. (2015). *Critical encounters in secondary English: Teaching literacy theory to adolescents* [eBook edition]. (3rd ed.). Teachers College Press.

AdLit. (n.d.). *Reading and writing strategies: Double-entry journals*. https://www.adlit.org/in-the-classroom/strategies/double-entry-journals

Aquino, K., & Khodos, G. (2020). Revolutionizing the canon: Repositioning texts during politically tumultuous times. In J. Dyches, B. Sams, & A. S. Boyd (Eds.), *Acts of resistance: Subversive teaching in the English language arts classroom* (pp. 212–224). Myers Education Press.

Bressler, C. E. (2007). *Literary criticism: An introduction to theory and practice* (4th ed.). Pearson.

Buell, L. (2001). *Writing for an endangered world: Literature, culture, and environment in the U.S. and beyond*. Harvard University Press.

Burke, J. (2013). *The English teacher's companion* (4th ed.). Heinemann.

Carson, R. (2002). *Silent spring*. Mariner Books.

Cesar Chavez Foundation. (n.d.). Speeches and writings. https://chavezfoundation.org/speeches-writings/#1549063588679-ed96425e-7969

Charles, D. (2021, January 20). *Toxic pesticide faces new scrutiny from Biden administration*.NPR.https://www.npr.org/sections/inauguration-day-live-updates/2021/01/20/958925222/toxic-pesticide-faces-new-scrutiny-from-biden-administration

Chavis, B. F., Jr. (1993). Foreword. In R. D. Bullard (Ed.), *Confronting environmental racism: Voices from the grassroots* (pp. 3–5). [Foreword]. South End Press.

Corchado, A. (2020, May 6). A former farmworker on American hypocrisy. *New York Times.* https://www.nytimes.com/2020/05/06/opinion/sunday/coronavirus-essential-workers.html

Crenshaw, K. W. (1991). Mapping the margins: Intersectionality, identity politics, and violence against women of color. *Stanford Law Review, 43*(6), 1241–1299.

Dakin, K. J., & Moyles, T. (2016, June 23). *Farmworkers push back against machismo and abuse in California's wine country.* The World from PRX. https://theworld.org/stories/2016/06/23/farmworkers-push-back-against-machismo-and-abuse-california-s-wine-country

Dobie, A. B. (2009). *Theory into practice: An introduction to literary criticism* (2nd ed.). Wadsworth Cengage Learning.

DonorsChoose. (n.d.). *Teacher sign-up.* https://www.donorschoose.org/teachers

Dyches, J. (2018). Shattering literary windows and mirrors: Creating prismatic canonical experiences for (and with) British literature students. In M. Macaluso & K. Macaluso (Eds.), *Teaching the canon in 21st century classrooms: Challenging genres* (pp. 35–49). Brill.

Freire, P. (2018). *Pedagogy of the oppressed.* Bloomsbury. (Original work published in 1970).

Garcia, A., & O'Donnell-Allen, C. (2015). *Pose, wobble, flow: A culturally proactive approach to literacy instruction.* Teachers College Press.

Gonzales, R. (2019, October 9). *California bans popular pesticide linked to brain damage in children.* NPR. https://www.npr.org/2019/10/09/768795666/california-bans-popular-pesticide-linked-to-brain-damage-in-children

Grewe-Volpp, C. (2005). "The oil was made from their bones": Environmental (in)justice in Helena María Viramontes's *Under the Feet of Jesus. Interdisciplinary Studies in Literature and Environment, 12*(1), 61–78.

GSA Network. (n.d.). *What is a GSA club?* https://gsanetwork.org/what-is-a-gsa/

Hanh, T. N. (2015). *The heart of the Buddha's teaching: Transforming suffering into peace, joy, and liberation.* Harmony.

Hines, C. M., & Penn, J. I. (2023). Seeing beyond the surface: Using critical lenses to combat anti-Blackness in the English classroom. *English Journal, 113*(1), 17–24.

hooks, b. (1994). *Teaching to transgress: Education as the practice of freedom*. Routledge.

Jordan, M. (2023, December 5). Retirement without a net: The plight of America's aging farmworkers. *New York Times*. https://www.nytimes.com/2023/12/05/us/aging-undocumented-farmworkers.html

Kirk, G. (1998). Ecofeminism and Chicano environmental struggles. In D. G. Peña (Ed.), *Chicano culture, ecology, politics: Subversive kin* (pp. 177–200). The University of Arizona Press.

Legler, G. T. (1997). Ecofeminist literary criticism. In K. Warren (Ed.), *Ecofeminism: Women, culture, nature* (pp. 227–238). Indiana University Press.

Lin, L., Parker, K., & Horowitz, J. M. (2024, April 4). *What's it like to be a teacher in America today?* Pew Research Center. https://www.pewresearch.org/social-trends/wp-content/uploads/sites/3/2024/04/ST_24.04.04_teacher-survey_report.pdf

López, D. (2014). "You talk 'merican?": Class, value, and the social production of difference in Helena María Viramontes's *Under the Feet of Jesus. College Literature, 41*(4), 41–70.

Luke, A. (2012). Critical literacy: Foundational notes. *Theory into Practice, 51*(4), 4–11. https://doi.org/10.1080/00405841.2012.636324

Morrell, E. (2008). *Critical literacy and urban youth: Pedagogies of access, dissent, and liberation*. Routledge.

Moses, M. (1993). Farmworkers and Pesticides. In R. D. Bullard (Ed.), *Confronting environmental racism: Voices from the grassroots* (pp. 161–178). South End Press.

National Council of Teachers of English. (2022, September 8). *Educators' right and responsibilities to engage in antiracist teaching*. https://ncte.org/statement/antiracist-teaching/

National Governors Association Center for Best Practices & Council of Chief State School Officers. (2010). *Common Core state standards for English language arts & literacy in history/social studies, science, and technical subjects*. Corestandards. https://www.thecorestandards.org/ELA-Literacy/

Planned Parenthood. (n.d.). *What does queer mean?* Plannedparenthood.org. https://www.plannedparenthood.org/learn/teens/sexual-orientation/what-doesqueer-mean

Rainey, E. C. (2017). Disciplinary literacy in English language arts: Exploring the social and problem-based nature of literary reading and reasoning. *Reading and Research Quarterly*, *52*(1), 53–71.

Romo, V. (2021, August 18). *EPA will ban a farming pesticide linked to health problems in children*. NPR. https://www.npr.org/2021/08/18/1029144997/epa-will-ban-a-farming-pesticide-linked-to-health-problems-in-children

Rosenblatt, L. (1978). *The reader, the text, the poem: The transactional theory of the literary work*. Southern Illinois University Press.

United Farm Workers. (n.d.). *The story of Cesar Chavez*. https://ufw.org/research/history/story-cesar-chavez/

Literature Cited

Viramontes, H. M. (1996). *Under the feet of Jesus*. Plume.

7

What Could Critical Literacy Pedagogy Look Like in Grade 12?

While this is not the case in every state or school district, many students in grade 12 in the United States study British literature their senior year of high school. For many grade 12 English language arts (ELA) teachers, the required British literature curriculum is almost "entirely White and male" (Dyches, 2018, p. 38). Today, many seniors, just like seniors before them, continue to study *Beowulf*; medieval romances; the works of Shakespeare; the poetry of Lord Byron, John Keats, and Percy Bysshe Shelley; and a novel or two, usually written by a White man.

ELA curricula for seniors based on an exclusionary canon can "function as tools for maintaining a marginalizing status quo" (Bissonnette & Glazier, 2016, p. 685). Teaching for CHANGE, though, aims to disrupt and dismantle the status quo. Harmful messages are communicated to young women, people of color, and otherwise marginalized or discriminated-against students when the majority of what they read and discuss in class excludes them and their experiences. Further, exclusionary canonical material "also negatively impacts students from mainstream groups by affirming and reproducing their privileges" (Dyches, 2018, p. 36) instead of helping them confront their privilege and supporting them in advocating for justice and equity for everyone. Therefore, it is important for those who teach grade 12 ELA to speak back to and against the traditional British literary canon.

Opportunities for Critical Literacy Pedagogy with Grade 12 Curriculum

The suggested unit detailed in the next section encourages you to use postcolonial literary theory to speak back to the traditional British literary canon. The unit I've created for this chapter is centered on Tsitsi Dangarembga's (2006) novel *The Book of Not*. Many teachers have mandated curricula that they must teach, so before I explain the unit, I will discuss some ways teachers can teach for CHANGE even with the current grade 12 curricula.

First, using critical literary theories like feminism and Marxism, teachers can use the canon in critical ways. For example, Mr. Tophill told me how he taught his seniors *Beowulf*: He facilitated class discussions inspired by feminist readings of the text. He and his students investigated what messages the epic communicated about masculinity and how the epic excluded the voices of women. The works of William Blake and Charles Dickens invite Marxist readings as both authors criticized industrialization and highlighted its consequences. Reading their works could spark discussions of child labor, minimum wage concerns, environmental justice issues, global warming, destructive mining practices to sustain our desire for new technology, and many other relevant topics. Please see the previous chapter for more information and suggested questions that can guide feminist and Marxist readings of literature.

In the previous chapter, I also mentioned ways that queer theory could influence the interpretation of texts taught in American literature courses. Some of those questions apply to queer readings of texts often taught in grade 12 curricula: "What sexual topics do you find in the work that are odd or peculiar—that is, queer?" and "Does the work show how sexual identities are indeterminate, overlapping, changing? If so, where?" (Dobie, 2009, p. 114). In the book *Queering the Middle Ages*, editors Burger and Kruger (2001) describe an approach that "'queers' [stabilized conceptions of medieval sexuality], allowing us to see the Middle Ages and its systems of sexuality in radically different, off-center, and revealing ways" (p. xiii). English professor Zeikowitz

(2002) argued that this approach to studying medieval texts allows readers to explore "peculiar" characters through a queer lens, even those who "cannot rightly be labeled 'gay'" (p. 67). Zeikowitz argued that Grendel (from *Beowulf*), the Green Knight (from *Sir Gawain and the Green Knight*), and the Pardoner (from *The Canterbury Tales*) are "all 'queer' in that they are not typical men of the time and, more significant, they all pose a challenge or threat to normative homosocial desire" (i.e., male bonding and intimacy that is not perceived as homosexual; p. 67).

In his article, Zeikowitz (2002) encourages English professors to guide their college students in queer readings of these characters to notice how they are ostracized because they do not conform to "socially acceptable male-male bonding and intimacy" (p. 71). Such analysis of these characters, Zeikowitz maintains, allows students to see that "both 'queerness' and 'normality' are not fixed terms; what is considered 'normal' at a particular sociohistorical moment may be considered queer at another time" (p. 71). For example, Zeikowitz points out that, in *Sir Gawain and the Green Knight*, Gawain and Lord Bertilak express "erotically charged affection" for each other as they embrace and kiss (p. 73), but they did so in ways that aligned with medieval homosocial normativity. Zeikowitz asserts their characters allow for a queer reading that invites an investigation into "contemporary, heteronormative" views in society (p. 74). Zeikowitz analyzed how the Pardoner's character in *The Canterbury Tales* "is constructed as a sexual being posing a threat to normative society and culturally defined masculine men" (p. 74). If I were teaching excerpts of *The Canterbury Tales*, I would use Zeikowitz's interpretation of the Pardoner's character to make connections to current ways that members of LGBTQIA+ communities are treated as threats. This could help my students read the word and the world critically and could make the study of a British medieval text more relevant to students' lives in the 21st century.

Obviously, your students are not college students yet, but *Beowulf*, chivalric and grail romances, and excerpts of *The Canterbury Tales* are often included in grade 12 curricula. If you are required to teach these canonical texts, you may find Zeikowitz's article instructive, and you can provide critical literacy pedagogy

(CLP) by teaching queer theory and guiding your students in queering these canonical texts and characters.

While the traditional British literary canon often emphasizes the works of White men, the canon does include some White women authors as well. As you are probably already doing, teachers can teach their works to emphasize feminist perspectives. Cook et al. (2018) recommend that teachers use Jane Austen's *Pride and Prejudice*, paired with Rowell's (2013) young adult novel *Eleanor & Park* to "foster critical conversation about gender and social class ideologies" (p. 155). Cook and colleagues argued that, because *Pride and Prejudice* offers a woman's perspective on marriage and the expectations placed on women, the novel's "themes provide opportunities to compare the normative social and gender expectations of the time period with the canonized norms of the present day" (p. 155). They recommend using the following questions to guide critical discussion of Austen and Rowell's novels: "To what extent should someone's family/social status define them?", "How important is it to fit in with the norms (e.g., social interaction, expectations for education and 'success,' etc.) of society? And what are those norms (who decides them)? What are the consequences of being 'different'?", and "How do our own prejudices influence our perceptions of the world? What about how others perceive us?" (p. 155). Cook and colleagues further encouraged teachers to connect the themes and issues of these novels with contemporary informational texts that address similar issues or concerns. Their suggested unit can work even within curricular restrictions that mandate certain texts be taught.

Another approach that promotes CLP is the practice of counterstorytelling (Bissonnette & Glazier, 2016). Bissonnette and Glazier's article highlights how using counterstorytelling helps students "talk back to the various issues of inequity manifest and perpetuated by the secondary literature curriculum" (p. 686). Counterstorytelling, as Bissonnette and Glazier explain, is based on Critical Race Theory (CRT). This approach values the power of narrative to speak back to inaccurate portrayals of marginalized groups and to create new understandings when everyone, not just the privileged few, is invited to share their stories. CRT scholar Richard Delgado (1989) argued that while "ideology – the received wisdom – makes current social arrangements seem fair and natural" (p. 2413), counterstories challenge that received wisdom and "can open new windows into reality, showing us that there are possibilities for life other than the ones we live" (p. 2414). If your mandated curriculum for students in grade 12 mostly emphasizes the voices of White, Anglo men, your curriculum is telling a story that promotes a certain ideology. It is likely the mandated curriculum makes the exclusion of other voices and stories—those told by women, people of color, and members of LGBTQIA+ communities—seem "fair and natural."

If you're still reading this book, you don't want to uphold that ideology. If you are required to teach certain texts, though, you may find yourself in a tough position: The curricular restrictions placed upon you are making teaching for CHANGE more challenging than it already is. Bissonnette and Glazier's (2016) suggestion to use counterstorytelling is an effective way to provide CLP even within restrictive curricular mandates. As they explain, counterstorytelling encourages students to "share their lived experiences" (p. 689) as they relate to the required texts being studied in class. Though this was only briefly mentioned in their article, I thought it was worth pointing out that when she taught Mary Shelley's *Frankenstein*, Bissonnette and her students explored how society "others" people who are different or who go against the status quo (p. 689). If you are required to teach that novel, you could create a unit that explores how society today treats people who do not fit within the status quo. This could be an excellent opportunity to explore the way that people who are transgender are being treated as monsters who must be controlled with restrictive laws and policies.

Bissonnette and Glazier (2016) used Virginia Woolf's essay *A Room of One's Own* to introduce students to the practice of counterstorytelling. In Woolf's essay, Bissonnette and Glazier explain, she provides a counterstory to the charge that women were intellectually inferior to men and therefore could not produce work of a quality similar to Shakespeare's. Woolf created the character Judith, Shakespeare's fictional sister, as a counterstory to argue "that the denial of education and extreme sexualization, both common and central experiences of the Renaissance woman, resulted in a reality in which women simply could not be Shakespeare" (Bissonnette & Glazier, p. 690). After a critical study of excerpts of *A Room of One's Own*, Bissonnette asked her students to use the essay as a model to write their own counterstories, and Bissonnette encouraged them to identify an ideology their counterstory would subvert. Her students wrote counterstories to address issues related to gender, race, ethnicity, and how young women of color are sexualized. Bissonnette and Glazier maintained that the practice of counterstorytelling "helps students develop the skills necessary to critique and talk back to systems of oppression–that is, develop their own sociopolitical consciousness" (p. 688), which is one of the goals of CLP.

Because Woolf's essay *A Room of One's Own* creates a fictional sister for Shakespeare, if you're required to teach Shakespeare, you can easily bring in an excerpt of Woolf's essay and teach lessons promoting the practice of counterstorytelling. Bissonnette and Glazier (2016) point out that Shakespeare's play *Othello* "grants students a rich opportunity to problematize issues of race and understand Othello's positionality" as a Black leader surrounded by White people who hold racist views of him (p. 691). They also suggest encouraging counterstorytelling with Geoffrey Chaucer's "The Wife of Bath's Tale" because it presents students with a counterstory to sexist medieval views of women. Using Zeikowitz's (2002) approach to interpreting the Pardoner in *The Canterbury Tales*, your students could write counterstories pushing back against heteronormativity. It is important to note that counterstorytelling can critique any abuse of power and injustice. Even though the practice grew out of CRT, counterstories do not have to be limited to issues of race and racism: All students have counterstories to tell. To help your students get the most out of this practice, Bissonnette and Glazier suggest that teachers give their students time to share their counterstories with the whole class. This allows students to learn with and from each other and to make deep connections with one another, even though they may come from different backgrounds, races, ethnicities, and cultures.

Overview of the Postcolonial Literature Unit for CHANGE

The suggested unit I describe below is meant to provide a counterstory to the traditional British literary canon. If you have the option to alter your grade 12 syllabus, I hope you'll consider implementing the Postcolonial Literature Unit for CHANGE. This unit focuses on postcolonial literary theory and has two main goals: (1) to dismantle the traditional British literary canon taught in high school ELA classrooms and (2) to use the study of a postcolonial text to engage students in exploring their futures, how they hope to obtain fulfillment and happiness, and what CHANGEs are needed to make a better world. The second goal connects to the themes of Dangarembga's novel *The Book of Not*, whose main character, Tambudzai, experiences disillusionment during her schooling and after graduating.

High school seniors will be able to connect with Tambudzai because they too are about to graduate into a world that might disappoint them and lead to their own disillusionment. I believe this novel is relevant to your students, even though it takes place in the 1970s at a time when many Zimbabweans were fighting for independence from White minority rule. In the 1970s, Zimbabwe was known as Rhodesia, named after Cecil Rhodes, a British colonizer who founded De Beers Jewellers (Parkinson, 2015).

I want to be clear: Dangarembga is a Zimbabwean novelist and activist. I am not arguing that her work should be viewed as British literature. It is a postcolonial Zimbabwean novel. Bressler (2007) defined postcolonial literature generally as "literature written in English in countries that were or still are colonies of other countries" (p. 235). Because of Britain's past colonization across the globe, I believe a "British Literature" course is the perfect space for a postcolonial literature unit. What is now Zimbabwe used to be a British colony, and Dangarembga writes in English. The main character Tambudzai attends a boarding school where the White nuns teach in English, the school operates under the British educational system, and Tambudzai's English classes use a traditional British literary canon. Tambudzai's younger sister chose to fight White minority rule, but Tambudzai seeks fulfillment in her schooling. Because of racist practices, though, Tambudzai's academic accomplishments are overlooked, and her White classmates receive the recognition and awards that Tambudzai is desperate to achieve and deserves.

Tambudzai graduates and acquires a job as a copywriter, and because of sexism and racism, a White man takes credit for her brilliant work and is recognized by the director of the advertising agency. Tambudzai quits her job, and the novel ends with Tambudzai pondering what is next for her in life and what is next for the new Zimbabwe as it gains independence. Again, I believe this is an excellent novel to use to teach postcolonial literary theory and to connect to the lives of your students, who are also likely asking themselves, "What's next?" It is unlikely that your school has a class set of *The Book of Not*, so if you decide to teach this unit, you might be able acquire funds to purchase copies using DonorsChoose (DonorsChoose, n.d.).

The Postcolonial Literature Unit Lesson Plans

The following lesson plans do not cover everything you would need to do to teach the novel *The Book of Not*. The lesson plans provided below focus on specific ways to teach for CHANGE. To accomplish the second goal of this unit (i.e., to engage students in exploring their futures, how they think they can obtain happiness, and what CHANGEs are needed to make a more just world), I suggest that you have your students research different approaches to accomplishing happiness. I also suggest that your students interview their peers, teachers, family members, and other influential adults in their lives to gain insights into how happiness and fulfillment can be achieved post-graduation. I consider their inquiry, research, and discussions to be crucial to this unit. Lesson Plan 10 below addresses this goal, but you will need more than one lesson to accomplish it. Your students can work on this inquiry and their research as they study the novel. I believe your students will benefit greatly from this unit as they Challenge injustice to Help make a difference in the world by Asking and answering tough questions and Noticing ways to Get involved and Engaged in making the world a better place.

The Postcolonial Literature Unit Lesson Plan 1

When to implement this lesson:	Before introducing the novel
Lesson objective:	Students will learn tenets of postcolonial theory and literary criticism.
Assessment:	Students will take notes on postcolonialism. Then, in groups, they will research two influential postcolonial scholars: Frantz Fanon and Edward Said. Students will participate in a class discussion of the contributions of these authors to postcolonialism.
Suggested texts needed:	A teacher-made handout summarizing notes on tenets and approaches to postcolonial literary analysis. Using the internet, students will need to conduct research on the works of Fanon and Said. You may find this website, which is maintained by Postcolonial Studies graduate students at Emory University, useful: https://scholarblogs.emory.edu/postcolonialstudies/ You can search for "Fanon, Frantz" and "Orientalism" in the top right corner to give your students online articles to read in their groups.
Suggested activities:	♦ Provide students with notes on postcolonialism. You can use the following points: ○ Colonization and colonialism not only used violence to "physically conquer territories" but also used "cultural colonization by replacing the practices and beliefs of the native culture with [the colonizers'] own values, governance, laws, and belief" (Dobie, 2009, p. 209). ○ Postcolonial literary criticism focuses on the works of postcolonial writers (i.e., those writers from formerly or currently colonized countries) as well as canonical texts written by Europeans to challenge the racism present in canonical works (Dobie). ○ European colonizers "assumed the superiority of their own culture and inferiority" of those belonging to the people they colonized; as a result, some of the people who were colonized came to believe they were inferior to Europeans (Dobie, p. 209). ○ Eurocentrism is the belief that European cultures were the "standard" against which other cultures were judged, and colonizers used this view to justify imposing their cultures on the people they colonized (Dobie, p. 209). ○ Colonizers practiced "othering," which is "viewing those who are different from oneself as inferior beings" (Dobie, p. 210).

(Continued)

- Bressler (2007) suggests these questions/approaches to guide a postcolonial literary analysis:
    - "What happens in the text when the two cultures clash, when one sees itself as superior to another?" (p. 243)
    - "Who in the text is 'the Other'?" (p. 243)
    - "What are the forms of resistance against colonial control?" (p. 243)
    - "How do the colonized people view themselves? Is there any change in this view by the end of the text?" (p. 243)
- Once students have taken notes on these approaches to analyzing literature, put them in groups and ask them to research either Fanon or Said's contributions to postcolonialism. Ask them to take notes to participate in a whole-class discussion.
- Then facilitate a class discussion on the influence of Fanon and Said on postcolonialism and the interpretive possibilities this critical theory has to offer readers. Even though I know you know how to lead class discussions, I like to share my suggestions in case you find them helpful:
    - Remind students of class rules and norms.
    - Print out example sentence starters and tape them to each student's desk so they can practice using the discourse valued in respectful discussions. For example, I might use some sentence starters they can use to participate in scholarly discourse. To help students state their opinion and defend it with evidence, they could use this sentence starter: "The author suggests [blank.] Notice what they wrote on page [blank]." To help students disagree respectfully, they could use this sentence starter: "That is one perspective, but I have a different one. What if we view it this way: [blank]?" To keep the discussion going, students could use this sentence starter: "What other perspectives are there, or who has something to say but has not been able to yet?"
- If time allows, have students reflect on their participation in the concluded discussion by answering questions like "How did I contribute to the class discussion? Did I contribute mostly by being a good listener, or did I contribute verbally or virtually to the discussion?" and "What would I do differently the next time we have a discussion?"

The Postcolonial Literature Unit Lesson Plan 2

When to implement this lesson:	Immediately after Lesson Plan 1
Lesson objective:	Students will read an essay by Chinua Achebe to analyze its argument and recognize how the essay aligns with and promotes postcolonial theory.
Assessment:	Students will annotate an informational text, and they will use their annotations to participate in a class discussion.
Suggested text needed:	♦ Achebe's (1975/2018) essay "An Image of Africa: Racism in Conrad's *Heart of Darkness*" *Warning: Achebe quotes Conrad's use of a racial slur for Black people in his essay.
Suggested activities:	♦ Introduce Achebe's essay by telling students he was a Nigerian author, critic, and professor whose work exposed "colonialist biases in [British] literature" and that he is internationally famous for his novel *Things Fall Apart*, which depicted the Igbo culture in Nigeria and "its clash with European culture" (Leitch et al., 2018, p. 1534). ♦ Then place students in small groups and ask them to read the essay together. Tell them their purpose in reading Achebe's essay is to discover what his main argument is. ♦ Once groups have had time to read and discuss together, ask them to pick one person to share their group's understanding of Achebe's main argument with the class. Facilitate a brief whole-class discussion of Achebe's main argument: Achebe's main argument is that though Joseph Conrad does critique European Imperialism, he represents Africans in racist ways in his novella. ♦ Then have students return to the essay in their groups. Ask them to identify how Achebe makes and supports his argument. Also ask them to identify some of the tenets of postcolonialism present in Achebe's essay. ♦ Facilitate a class discussion on how Achebe supports his argument and what tenets of postcolonialism are present in his essay.

The Postcolonial Literature Unit Lesson Plan 3

When to implement this lesson:	After students have read the first four chapters
Lesson objective:	To help students produce a postcolonial analysis of the novel in Lesson Plan 9, this lesson will focus students' attention on ways that Tambudzai and her Black roommates are othered in the novel.
Assessment:	Students will reread and discuss key scenes of the novel so far.
Suggested texts needed:	No additional texts needed
Suggested activities:	♦ Place students into small groups. Ask the groups to reread the following pages to address the questions from Lesson Plan 1 that can guide a postcolonial reading: 　o Page 45: Tambudzai considers the quota imposed by the Rhodesian government for the maximum percentage of students at the convent school who may be Black Africans instead of White or European. 　o Pages 47–48: Tambudzai's roommate Ntombi asks a White classmate at lunch for some of her powdered chocolate so she could make herself some chocolate milk. 　o Pages 61 and 72: Tambudzai contemplates the energy and effort that she and her Black roommates put into making sure they do not physically touch their White classmates or teachers because it is against the rules. 　o Page 63: Tambudzai describes the "African dormitory." 　o Pages 77–78: The girls in the African dormitory are blamed for clogging the sewer system at the boarding school. In these pages, Tambudzai reflects on her intersectionality as an African young woman with a different skin color from most of the students. 　o Pages 79–83: Tambudzai uses a restroom intended to be used only by White students and is caught. ♦ Give students time to discuss the passages in their small groups. Encourage them to make connections to their own lives and relevant issues in society. (For example, students may discuss how students of color are underrepresented in "gifted-and-talented" classes in many schools, and students may discuss ways that intersectionality affects their lives; for a definition and discussion of intersectionality, see Crenshaw, 1991.) Require them to take notes on their group's conclusions and connections. ♦ Then engage students in a whole-class discussion of the first four chapters of the novel.

The Postcolonial Literature Unit Lesson Plan 4

When to implement this lesson:	Immediately after Lesson Plan 3
Lesson objective:	Students will read a short story through a postcolonial lens to produce a postcolonial analysis of the text.
Assessment:	Students will write short literary analysis essays.
Suggested text needed:	South African author and activist Nadine Gordimer's short story titled, "The Train from Rhodesia"
Suggested activities:	♦ Ask students to read the short story on their own and use the rest of class to write a literary analysis of the text using a postcolonial lens. You may need to remind them of this question that can guide their analysis: "What happens in the text when the two cultures clash, when one sees itself as superior to another?" (Bressler, 2007, p. 243). You can also encourage them to ask these questions: Which characters see themselves as superior? Why? Finally, you may also want to encourage students to look for ways the passengers on the train othered the Black venders. ♦ Encourage students to share their essays with each other.

The Postcolonial Literature Unit Lesson Plan 5

When to implement this lesson:	After reading Chapter 9
Lesson objective:	Students will continue to analyze *The Book of Not* using the tenets and approaches of postcolonialism to guide their analysis.
Assessment:	Students will take notes on ways they can analyze the novel through a postcolonial lens.
Suggested texts needed:	You may want to have copies of Emily Brontë's *Wuthering Heights*, or students can use the internet to look up summaries of the novel.
Suggested activities:	♦ Review the novel and postcolonialism as needed, making sure to emphasize how Tambudzai's academic achievement was unfairly overlooked. ♦ Point out to students that Tambudzai's English course emphasizes the works of White British authors like Shakespeare and Emily Brontë (see page 176). Encourage students to read a summary of *Wuthering Heights*, if you have not already taught it to them, and to discuss how the ways Heathcliff is treated could connect to Tambudzai's experiences at school.

(Continued)

	♦ Then facilitate a class discussion on how Tambudzai's school practices engaged in cultural domination and the impact this had on Tambudzai and how she thought of herself and her Black roommates. ♦ Ask students to take notes during the discussion to help them write a literary analysis of the novel in a future lesson.

The Postcolonial Literature Unit Lesson Plan 6

When to implement this lesson:	After reading Chapter 10
Lesson objective:	Students will learn about the concept of "uplift suasion."
Assessment:	Students will participate in a class discussion and will take notes during their discussion to help them write a literary analysis of the novel in a future lesson.
Suggested texts needed:	You may want to have students read excerpts of Ibram X. Kendi's (2017) *Stamped from the Beginning: The Definitive History of Racist Ideas in America* or of Kendi's (2019) *How to be an Antiracist*.

Suggested activities:	♦ Begin the lesson by defining "uplift suasion":
	   o Uplift suasion is the idea that people who are racialized and discriminated against because of their race need to "prove their worthiness" to people who hold racist ideas (Kendi, 2017, p. 154), so it blames those who are racialized as if they deserve to be viewed and treated as inferior.
	   o People who adhere to uplift suasion believe that by adjusting their conduct, by improving their education, and by moving upward economically, they can convince those who hold racist views to stop (Kendi, 2017). Uplift suasion encourages people to believe, as Kendi once did, that "good Black behavior made White people 'less racist'" (Kendi, 2019, p. 204).
	   o An antiracist perspective counters uplift suasion and argues that associating an individual person's behavior with their race is a racist view (Kendi, 2019).
	♦ Next, remind students that a postcolonial analysis of a text would examine the way the colonizers culturally dominated those whom they colonized as well as the effects such treatment had on the ways the colonized people viewed themselves.

(Continued)

	♦ Then place students into small groups. You will need at least four groups. Assign each group some pages of *The Book of Not* to reread now that they have learned about uplift suasion. Require students to discuss how Tambudzai's thoughts and experiences connect to the concept of uplift suasion: ○ Group 1: Pages 87 and 125: Tambudzai is angry with her Black roommates for embarrassing her because they disposed of their menstrual pads in the toilet (see page 77). Tambudzai thinks about doing well in her studies and becoming gainfully employed so that one day her country could be viewed as an inspiration (p. 125). ○ Group 2: Pages 137–139: Tambudzai plans to become the top-scoring student and prove to her classmates how smart she is. ○ Group 3: Pages 168–169 and 183: Ntombi and Tambudzai almost fight in the dorm, and their roommates tell them to stop so that the Europeans don't think the girls from the "African dormitory" resort to physical violence all the time. ○ Group 4: Pages 183–185 and 199: After Tambudzai and Ntombi performed well on a standardized test (p. 183) ♦ Facilitate the class discussion on uplift suasion and how the novel can be interpreted using postcolonialism. Ask students to take notes during the discussion.

The Postcolonial Literature Unit Lesson Plan 7

When to implement this lesson:	After reading Chapter 12
Lesson objectives:	Students will read online articles about Cecil Rhodes and controversies surrounding him. Students will discuss what they learned, how it connects to *The Book of Not*, and how controversies over statues of Rhodes relate to similar controversies in the United States.
Assessment:	Students will write summaries of informational texts and participate in a class discussion.
Suggested texts needed:	Two online articles, both published by BBC News (the links are in the references at the end of this chapter): ♦ Parkinson's (2015) "Why is Cecil Rhodes Such a Controversial Figure?" ♦ Race's (2021) "Cecil Rhodes Statue Will Not Be Removed by Oxford College"

(Continued)

Suggested activities:	♦ Place students into pairs. Assign one student the Parkinson (2015) article and assign the other student the Race (2021) article. ♦ Ask students to take notes on the articles so they can summarize them for their partner. ♦ Encourage the students to share their summaries and ask each other questions to make sure they have reviewed the key information from both articles. ♦ Facilitate a class discussion on Cecil Rhodes, the controversy over statues of him, and connections to both the novel and similar controversies in the United States.

The Postcolonial Literature Unit Lesson Plan 8[1]

When to implement this lesson:	Immediately after Lesson Plan 7
Lesson objective:	Students will hear a counterstory to the White supremacist perspective that African nations need White people to rule them.
Assessment:	Students will write a counterstory, either to the racist perspectives regarding African nations or to another narrative they wish to speak back to.
Suggested texts needed:	♦ Beauchamp's (2015) article titled "The Racist Flags on Dylann Roof's Jacket, Explained," published by Vox Media. The link is in the references at the end of this chapter. ♦ Excerpts of Burgis's (2015) book *The Looting machine: Warlords, Oligarchs, Corporations, Smugglers, and the Theft of Africa's Wealth* (the first few pages of Chapter 10, for example, discuss the corrupt deeds of the former ruler of Zimbabwe, the autocrat Robert Mugabe, who ruled from 1980 to 2017) ♦ A video posted on YouTube by CaspianReport (2018), titled "Review: *The Looting Machine* by Tom Burgis"
Suggested activities:	♦ Because your students might not know about Dylann Roof, the White supremacists who murdered nine Black people at their church in Charleston, South Carolina, in 2015, start the lesson by warning them of the serious nature of the topics covered in this lesson and by reviewing that tragedy. ♦ Then ask students to read and annotate Beauchamp's (2015) article.

(Continued)

- ◆ Next, facilitate a brief discussion of the article's main points, making sure to emphasize that Roof wore a patch of Rhodesia's flag on his jacket and to highlight the White supremacist view that African people are inferior to White people and that White people should rule African nations. Help them see that this is one, racist story or narrative of African nations.
- ◆ Then show students the CaspianReport (2018) video. You may also want to have students read excerpts from Burgis's book *The Looting Machine*. These texts present a counterstory to the White supremacist view. They explain the economic troubles of many African nations as resulting from corruption and greed, perpetuated by individuals and corporations.
- ◆ Facilitate a class discussion on the texts and the counterstory they offer.
- ◆ Once students have discussed the counterstory, have them write their own. They can choose to write the counterstory presented by Burgis's book, or they may want to write a counterstory dismantling a story that has been told about them.

The Postcolonial Literature Unit Lesson Plan 9

When to implement this lesson:	After students have finished reading the novel
Lesson objective:	Students will analyze the novel using a postcolonial lens.
Assessment:	Students will write a literary analysis of the novel.
Suggested texts needed:	No additional texts needed
Suggested activities:	◆ Review the notes on postcolonialism from Lesson Plan 1. ◆ Give students time to brainstorm what evidence they need from the novel to write their essays. Facilitate class discussion if needed. ◆ You may want to direct students' attention to the following passages toward the end of the novel: 　○ Page 250: At the single ladies' hostel, the White matron confuses Tambudzai with another Black resident. 　○ Page 292: Dick Lawson, a White man who took credit for Tambudzai's copy, receives the award that Tambudzai should have received.

	○ Page 297: The final page of the novel when Tambudzai wonders about her future after she quit her job and has been asked to move out of the single ladies' hostel. She ponders the future of Zimbabwe.
	♦ Then support students as needed in composing and revising their literary analysis essays.

The Postcolonial Literature Unit Lesson Plan 10

When to implement this lesson:	After students have finished reading the novel
Lesson objectives:	Students will review Tambudzai's attempts to achieve happiness and fulfillment as well as times when she became disillusioned. They will continue to conduct research on ways they can pursue their own happiness and fulfillment—including ways they can effect CHANGE so that they will graduate into a more just world.
Assessment:	Students will select and plan a way to engage in effective activism.
Suggested texts needed:	Any texts students have decided to read based on their research.

Suggested activities:	♦ Place students into small groups to analyze how and why Tambudzai became increasingly disillusioned in the novel.
	♦ You may want to assign them specific passages to review:
	  ○ Pages 100–101: Tambudzai thinks about how bright her future is because she will do well in school.
	  ○ Page 138: Tambudzai plans to score the highest in her class on a standardized test so that her name will be placed on a trophy.
	  ○ Page 188: The trophy Tambudzai worked so hard for is awarded to a White student who had a lower score than she.
	  ○ Page 222: Tambudzai receives her grades, and they are poor.
	  ○ Page 234: After graduating, Tambudzai works a few jobs she is not proud of, and she becomes discouraged.
	  ○ Page 292: Dick Lawson receives the award that Tambudzai deserves for her copy that he took credit for.
	  ○ Page 294: After Tambudzai quits her job at the advertising agency, she thinks about how she cannot tell her mother what has happened because she feels like a failure.

> - ♦ Facilitate a discussion of what Tambudzai thought would bring her happiness and fulfillment, what got in the way of her achieving her goals (e.g., racism, sexism, colonialism, and conflicts between the government and those fighting for independence), and what contributed to her disillusionment.
> - ♦ Then, as time allows in your curriculum, support students as they continue to research what they think can bring them fulfillment and how they can make the world more just and equitable.
>
> Because of time and curricular demands, you may need to have them continue to work on this inquiry project as you begin another unit of study.

Anticipated Moments of Wobble with the Postcolonial Literature Unit

One thing that would certainly cause me wobble with this unit is the emphasis on postcolonialism. Sadly, many politically conservative legislators and parents and guardians mistakenly believe that addressing racism is itself racist. They are busy trying to make laws to protect White students from "feeling guilty" because of their race, and they are working to ban books that deal with the very issues that postcolonialism highlights. If you live in a state like Florida, I believe it would be difficult to teach the Postcolonial Literature Unit and still keep your job (see Simonson, 2022). I don't want to encourage anyone to do anything that would cause them to be terminated. If you're still reading this book, you're the kind of teacher this world needs. So please continue to provide CLP, even if you must do so subversively and can't do something as openly critical as the Postcolonial Literature Unit, so that your students can still engage in critical literacy themselves.

Anticipated Moments of Wobble with Specific Lesson Plans

The first two lesson plans could cause wobble because they introduce students to postcolonialism and help them understand how to interpret texts using a postcolonial lens. As you teach these lessons, you may fear being accused of indoctrinating youth or of "teaching CRT." The previous two chapters have addressed this potential wobble, so I will address this only briefly here: Teaching students critical literary theories is something ELA teachers are expected to do (Appleman, 2015), and it sets students up for success in their college English courses (see Rainey, 2017). If parents or guardians do complain, you can help them see that this unit is rigorous and beneficial for their children.

Lesson Plans 3, 4, and 5 all focus specifically on how to conduct postcolonial interpretations of texts. Therefore, I imagine that these lessons could cause wobble for reasons already addressed. If you are experiencing wobble because of these lessons, please remember that Dangarembga's novel takes place in the 1970s in Zimbabwe. It would be difficult for a White parent or guardian to argue convincingly that your instruction is meant to make their child feel guilty when the novel is set half a century ago in a different country.

The sixth lesson plan is the one that would probably cause me the most wobble if I were to teach it today. An exploration of uplift suasion with students could lead to heated discussions. Also, some of Kendi's books have been banned by politically conservative school districts (see Donovan & Gregory, 2023). If this lesson is causing you serious anticipatory wobble, remember that investigating what Tambudzai thinks about herself is part of analyzing her character, a valued literacy practice in ELA.

The heavy topics like White supremacy covered in Lesson Plans 7 and 8 might also cause you some wobble. These topics could spark heated discussions and could elicit problematic statements from students. Additionally, because Lesson Plan 8 encourages students to write counterstories, which grew out of CRT, some might accuse you of "teaching CRT" in these lessons. One thing that could alleviate your wobble is that Rhodes is not a United States "hero," so it is less likely students, parents, and guardians would be upset about the removal of his statues. Also, Lesson Plan 8 counters a White supremacist perspective; I hope none of your students or their parents and guardians upholds White supremacist views.

The wobble that Lesson Plan 9 could cause has already been discussed, so that leaves the final suggested lesson plan. I did not experience much wobble when creating Lesson Plan 10. Focusing on Tambudzai's disillusionment helps make the novel more relevant to your students who will soon leave secondary school to pursue their futures. Encouraging them to research what they think will lead to their future happiness and fulfillment is relevant, engaging, and promising. It helps students take action to pursue their interests and passion. I do not believe any reasonable parent or guardian could complain about what this lesson hopes to accomplish.

Encouragement to Expand Your Stretchiness

If you think you may wobble if you taught this unit, I want to encourage you to use the wobble you'll experience as an opportunity to expand your stretchiness. I want to encourage you to teach this unit even though it causes you discomfort. In general, my suggestions are the same for each recommended unit for grades 9, 10, 11, and 12: (1) collaborate with your English teacher peers, school administrators, and parents/guardians; (2) adjust the unit as you see fit for your classroom; (3) create a rationale you can use to defend your pedagogical decisions; and (4) spend some time reflecting on what your wobble can teach you about yourself.

Collaborate with Your English Teacher Peers, School Administrators, and Parents/Guardians

As I've recommended throughout this book, please work with your colleagues who teach the same courses you do. Together, you can improve the lesson plans to make them more appropriate for your school. As a group, you can create activities that are more engaging than the ones I've come up with, and you can collaborate to create a rationale or revise the recommended letter to parents and guardians I've included in the Appendices (see Appendix E). Your individual experiences with wobble will likely be easier for you to address and grow from if you know you're not alone.

Another benefit of collaborating is that together you can plan how to address your school administrators with your plans for the Postcolonial Literature Unit. Together, you can decide how to get your administration to support your pedagogical decisions (and purchase copies of *The Book of Not* perhaps?). I believe that your administrators want to support you, so work together to help them understand how they can do that.

While fear of repercussions caused from angering parents and guardians was the main source of Mrs. Skipmann and Ms. Wilson's wobbles when they participated in my study, the parents and guardians of your students deserve to know what you're doing in your class. They deserve the opportunity to support their teens and you as the teacher. Parents and guardians want their teens to graduate and become happy and fulfilled adults. I suggest that you communicate with them about what you're trying to accomplish with this unit. If you help them appreciate the value of the Postcolonial Literature Unit, they can support their teens in planning how to achieve happiness and fulfillment in life. I think this would be a wonderful opportunity for parents and guardians to spend time together with their teens before they graduate.

Adjust the Unit

Garcia and O'Donnell-Allen (2015) compared experiencing wobble to practicing yoga. I return to their metaphor each time I think about adjusting the units I've suggested in this book. If you practice yoga, you know that attempting a new pose can be very challenging and equally as rewarding once you've accomplished it. You know that you were able to accomplish the new pose by making the needed adjustments early on until you developed the needed strength in the right muscles and the necessary balance and confidence. If you're a yoga practitioner, you know that with time, practice, and the right approach, you can accomplish new and increasingly challenging poses.

This metaphor applies to the Postcolonial Literature Unit: It is a new "pose," and you might have to adjust how you attempt it, at least at first. This unit could be challenging, especially if you live in a state that is passing laws to silence classroom discourse on racism. You can adjust the unit, so that one day you may feel stretchy enough to accomplish it as described in this chapter. Instead of not attempting the Postcolonial Literature Unit altogether, please consider adjusting it the first time you teach it.

For example, if you think you'll experience too much wobble to handle right now regarding the concept of uplift suasion, you can still teach most of the unit. Simply eliminate Lesson Plan 6. You can still help students analyze Tambudzai's character and how colonization has affected her self-concept without specifically mentioning Kendi or uplift suasion.

If you're experiencing wobble because you're afraid you'll be accused of "teaching CRT" when you ask students to write counterstories, you can still teach all the lessons in this unit. Just don't use the term "counterstory." You can say that students will write their own stories, and leave it at that. I want to be clear: I don't advocate that you lie. You should always be honest about what you're doing in the classroom. At the same time, if people are so dedicated to their ill-informed ideologies that they don't take the time to understand something before they criminalize it, I'm not going to apologize for choosing my words carefully. Counterstorytelling is not a harmful practice. It is a useful practice for all students and makes what they study in class relevant to their lives. If you think people in your community will object to "counterstorytelling" because of its roots in CRT, call it something else while being honest about what the assignment asks students to do.

Regardless of what might cause you to wobble if you teach this unit, please make the adjustments you and your colleagues deem fit. Please give it a chance. You and your students might learn a lot about yourselves and each other as you work to make the needed CHANGEs so your students can graduate into a world that is more conducive to their and others' happiness and fulfillment.

Create a Rationale

If you decide to teach the Postcolonial Literature Unit (even after making the necessary adjustments), you will probably be better prepared to address wobbles you'll experience if you create a rationale. Creating a rationale may help you teach this unit, and doing so can expand your stretchiness, which will help you with future wobbles you're bound to experience in your teaching career. Coming up with a rationale will require you to articulate why you think the unit is valuable and to plan how you can communicate that to your colleagues, administrators, students and their parents and guardians. This can help you address issues as they arise. I also suggest that you remind yourself of your teaching philosophy and what you feel is most important in ELA instruction. As you think about your rationale, here are some points to consider:

- ♦ As I've now written in the two previous chapters, if you are concerned about accusations that you are "teaching CRT," you can defend yourself by reading and citing the National Council of Teachers of English's (NCTE's) position statement titled, "Educators' Right and Responsibilities to Engage in Antiracist Teaching" (NCTE, 2022).
- ♦ For decades, educators have recognized the importance of increasing the diversity of school ELA curricula so that students have the opportunity both to see themselves reflected in the curricula and to learn about people with different backgrounds and experiences from their own (see Sims Bishop, 1990). The traditional British literature curricula taught in the United States do not offer enough of those opportunities to the increasingly diverse student populations attending high school (Bissonnette & Glazier, 2016). This unit diversifies the grade 12 ELA curriculum, and the themes of Dangarembga's *The Book of Not* are relevant to high school seniors who themselves may be looking for happiness and fulfillment in their academic achievement or in their employment.
- ♦ Your students are seniors, and so they should be mature enough to participate in serious discussions of heavy topics. Even states like Florida, where there are restrictive laws regarding classroom discourse, allow for discussions of racism in "age appropriate" ways (Simonson, 2022). Your seniors are old enough to handle the Postcolonial Literature Unit.

I've written an example letter you could send to parents or guardians to let them know about your plans for the Postcolonial Literature Unit (see Appendix E). You are welcome to use the entire letter, but you will need to include the correct contact information.

Spend Time Reflecting

While I've discussed some moments of wobble I think you might experience if you implement the Postcolonial Literature Unit, each person experiences wobble differently. As you know, moments of wobble can produce feelings of intense discomfort and fear. In his book *The Heart of the Buddha's Teaching: Transforming Suffering into Peace, Joy, and Liberation*, the late Buddhist monk Thich Nhat Hanh discusses the importance of mindfully acknowledging our feelings without judgment. Hanh (2015) wrote, "when our feelings are stronger than our mindfulness, we suffer" (p. 73). If you're wobbling as you consider implementing this unit, that's okay! Your wobble does not have to make you suffer. Take some time to reflect on what your feelings are telling you about your teaching practice and about yourself as a human. What are they telling you about your personal and professional needs? Look deeply into them, without judging yourself or allowing the feelings to take over your mind. I hope you'll find that pausing and reflecting gives you perspective and produces wisdom that you can apply to your teaching practice.

Note

1 Because this lesson addresses White supremacist views and mass murder, please warn your students in advance of the serious nature of the topics and issues being studied and discussed in class.

References

Achebe, C. (2018). An image of Africa: Racism in Conrad's *Heart of Darkness*. In V. B. Leitch, W. E. Cain, L. A. Finke, J. McGowan, T. D. Sharpley-Whiting, & J. J. Williams (Eds.), *The Norton anthology of theory and criticism* (3rd ed., pp. 1536–1546). Norton.

Appleman, D. (2015). *Critical encounters in secondary English: Teaching literacy theory to adolescents* [eBook edition]. (3rd ed.). Teachers College Press.

Beauchamp, Z. (2015, June 18). *The racist flags on Dylann Roof's jacket, explained*.Vox.https://www.vox.com/2015/6/18/8806633/charleston-shooter-flags-dylann-roof

Bissonnette, J. D., & Glazier, J. (2016). A counterstory of own's own: Using counterstorytelling to engage students with the British canon. *Journal of Adolescent and Adult Literacy, 59*(6), 685–694.

Bressler, C. E. (2007). *Literary criticism: An introduction to theory and practice* (4th ed.). Pearson.

Burger, G., & Kruger, S. F. (Eds.). (2001). *Queering the middle ages*. University of Minnesota Press.

Burgis, T. (2015). *The looting machine: Warlords, oligarchs, corporations, smugglers, and the theft of Africa's wealth*. PublicAffairs.

CaspianReport. (2018, August 31). *Review: The Looting Machine by Tom Burgis* [Video]. *YouTube*. https://www.youtube.com/watch?v=oRMDMNSsTDU&t=29s

Cook, M. P., Sams, B. L., & Wade, P. (2018). Interrupting ideologies withing the canon: Applying critical lenses to *Pride and Prejudice, Eleanor & Park*, and contemporary life. In M. Macaluso & K. Macaluso (Eds.), *Teaching the canon in 21st century classrooms: Challenging genres* (pp. 151–164). Brill.

Crenshaw, K. W. (1991). Mapping the margins: Intersectionality, identity politics, and violence against women of color. *Stanford Law Review, 43*(6), 1241–1299.

Delgado, R. (1989). Storytelling for oppositionists and others: A plea for narrative. *Michigan Law Review, 87*(8), 2411–2441.

Dobie, A. B. (2009). *Theory into practice: An introduction to literary criticism* (2nd ed.). Wadsworth Cengage Learning.

DonorsChoose. (n.d.). *Teacher sign-up*. https://www.donorschoose.org/teachers

Donovan, S., & Gregory, S. (2023, April 27). *1st legal challenge to recent SC book bans comes from Pickens County*. Post and Courier. https://www.postandcourier.com/greenville/news/1st-legal-challenge-to-recent-sc-book-bans-comes-from-pickens-county/article_9d41748c-e519-11ed-8ca1-df5cba9cbc1f.html

Dyches, J. (2018). Shattering literary windows and mirrors: Creating prismatic canonical experiences for (and with) British literature students. In M. Macaluso & K. Macaluso (Eds.), *Teaching the canon in 21st century classrooms: Challenging genres* (pp. 35–49). Brill.

Garcia, A., & O'Donnell-Allen, C. (2015). *Pose, wobble, flow: A culturally proactive approach to literacy instruction*. Teachers College Press.

Hanh, T. N. (2015). *The heart of the Buddha's teaching: Transforming suffering into peace, joy, and liberation*. Harmony.

Kendi, I. X. (2017). *Stamped from the beginning: The definitive history of racist ideas in America*. Bold Type Books.

Kendi, I. X. (2019). *How to be an antiracist*. One World.

Leitch, V. B., Cain, W. E., Finke, L. A., McGowan, J., Sharpley-Whiting, T. D., & Williams, J. J. (Eds.). (2018). *The Norton anthology of theory and criticism* (3rd ed.). Norton.

National Council of Teachers of English. (2022, September 8). *Educators' right and responsibilities to engage in antiracist teaching*. https://ncte.org/statement/antiracist-teaching/

Parkinson, J. (2015, April 1). *Why is Cecil Rhodes such a controversial figure?* BBC News. https://www.bbc.com/news/magazine-32131829

Race, M. (2021, May 20). *Cecil Rhodes statue will not be removed by Oxford college*. BBC News. https://www.bbc.com/news/uk-england-oxfordshire-57175057

Rainey, E. C. (2017). Disciplinary literacy in English language arts: Exploring the social and problem-based nature of literary reading and reasoning. *Reading and Research Quarterly*, *52*(1), 53–71.

Simonson, A. (2022, January 20). *Florida bill to shield people from feeling "discomfort" over historic actions by their race, nationality or gender approved by Senate committee*. CNN. https://www.cnn.com/2022/01/19/us/florida-education-critical-race-theory-bill/index.html

Sims Bishop, R. (1990). Mirrors, windows, and sliding glass doors. *Perspectives*, *6*(3), ix–xi.

Zeikowitz, R. E. (2002). Befriending the medieval queer: A pedagogy for literature classes. *College English*, *65*(1), 67–80.

Literature Cited

Dangarembga, T. (2006). *The book of not*. Graywolf Press.

Rowell, R. (2013). *Eleanor & park*. Macmillan.

8

Conclusion

The previous four chapters have provided suggestions for ways you can teach for CHANGE. I hope you've found the suggested units in each of those chapters useful. More importantly, I hope this book has inspired you to continue working with your colleagues at your school to create even better units than the ones I've included. As you continue providing critical literacy pedagogy (CLP), you will experience wobble (i.e., tension, fear, dread, and doubt). Therefore, in this concluding chapter, I wanted to provide three additional suggestions that I hope will encourage you to continue teaching for CHANGE.

Practice Mindfulness

From a Buddhist perspective, practicing mindfulness is essential for humans to connect to the deepest realities of the universe and to stop the cycle of suffering in the world. According to the late Buddhist monk Thich Nhat Hanh (2015), *mindfulness* is "remembering to come back to the present moment" (p. 64). You don't have to understand the mysteries of the universe, and you are not individually responsible for ending suffering in the world, but there are benefits to practicing mindfulness that anyone can enjoy, anytime. You don't have to be a Buddhist to enjoy these benefits.

One benefit is that mindfulness allows us to accept what we are experiencing but without "judging or reacting" (Hanh, 2015, p. 64). A second benefit is that, through mindfulness, we can understand our emotions better. If we investigate those emotions, we can understand our needs and values more deeply (see Richo, 1991; Rosenberg, 2015). With this deeper understanding, we can take care of our emotions without letting them take over us. Another benefit of mindfulness, therefore, is that it allows us to be focused when we make decisions.

You can practice mindfulness—even while teaching the final period of a hot day in June—through mindful breathing. As Hanh explained, mindful breathing involves thinking a specific thought during an inhale and another specific thought during an exhale of the breath. This practice allows us to "embrace all of our feelings, even difficult ones like anger" (Hanh, p. 72). Hanh recommends the following template for embracing difficult emotions: "Breathing in, I calm my anger. Breathing out, I take care of my anger" (p. 72). Adjusting that template slightly, you can practice mindful breathing when you experience wobble: "Breathing in, I recognize I'm wobbling. Breathing out, I know I can handle the wobble." When you're teaching a lesson and something causes you to wobble in the moment, just take a second to breathe mindfully.

If you're planning a lesson or unit that is causing you to wobble, take advantage of the time you have before you're in the middle of teaching it to reflect mindfully. Embrace the emotions that arise as you experience wobble. Ask yourself questions like "Why am I wobbling? What emotions am I feeling? What does this say about me and my beliefs/values? What good thing does this wobble tell me about myself as a human and as a teacher?" Mindfully reflecting on these questions can help you grow personally and professionally.

For wobble to be valuable to you, you must respond to it mindfully (Fecho et al., 2005; Garcia & O'Donnell-Allen, 2015). You won't grow from wobbling if you constantly avoid it or if you allow the emotions it creates to control you. Practicing mindfulness can help you remain in control of your emotions and can give you insight into how to respond to your wobble productively so that you can grow from it and expand your stretchiness for future wobbles. Remember, to expand your stretchiness (i.e., your readiness and commitment to providing CLP) for future wobbles, you'll need to be focused and in control when you respond to it, and mindfulness can help you do that.

Practice Compassion for Yourself and Those around You

Another way to respond productively to your wobbles is to practice compassion for yourself. Remember Csikszentmihalyi's (1990) concept of *flow*—the amazing experiences that come from pursuing a challenging but obtainable goal that make life meaningful? Flow is closely related to mindfulness, for they both emphasize the importance of pairing action with reflection so you can make better decisions that increase your chances of accomplishing your goals. Another important part of flow is a person's control or agency. To obtain flow, a person must have some control: They must be able to set the goal and plan how to accomplish it, and they must have the agency to pursue it and decide how to address challenges as they arise.

When you're trying to teach for CHANGE and you wobble, you're encountering a challenge. This means that wobble is an opportunity for you to obtain flow. When you pursue the worthwhile goal of enacting CLP, you can achieve flow, even in the very moment that you're also experiencing intense wobble. To achieve flow as you wobble, though, you need agency. This is why it is important to practice compassion for yourself.

You can extend compassion to yourself by recognizing what you have control over and what you don't. If you're teaching in a state that has criminalized some approaches to CLP, please give yourself some compassion. You might not be able to teach any of the units I've suggested in this book and keep your job. Please don't judge yourself for the wobbles you experience or for the realities of life that are beyond your control. Of course, I hope you'll still find ways to teach for CHANGE subversively, but I would hate for you to condemn yourself because of things outside your control. States with restrictive laws that control classroom discourse need teachers like you who are passionate about critical literacy, so please continue to expand your stretchiness for wobble (whatever that means for you in your context) and please continue teaching for CHANGE as best as you can. Garcia and O'Donnell-Allen (2015) pointed out that wobble is natural and is a good sign: It means you're doing something meaningful and worthwhile. When you wobble, don't judge or condemn yourself. Practice compassion for self.

The more compassionate you can be with yourself, the more compassion you'll be able to extend toward those around you. When your students say something harmful and problematic in response to your instruction, try to extend compassion toward them. They are likely just repeating something they heard from another source, and they probably haven't thought through the impact their words have on their peers. Your students need you to respond to them compassionately as you correct them and help them see how what they said was problematic. If you can't extend compassion toward yourself, I doubt you'll be able to give much compassion to your students. You and they deserve compassion.

It is extremely upsetting if a parent or guardian complains to you or about you to your administrators. I have experienced this myself. I imagine you have too. If a parent or guardian expresses their complaint using violent or threatening language, please contact your school administrators immediately. I hope they'll give you the support you deserve, as threats of violence are never acceptable. I don't really think you need to extend much compassion to someone expressing violence toward you. In my eight years of teaching high schoolers, though, no parent or guardian ever threatened me.

I believe most parents and guardians who complain because you've enacted CLP are doing so out of a genuine concern for their children. Most of the parents and guardians who will complain are doing so because they have certain values they feel are being challenged by your instruction, and they are concerned that your teaching will negatively impact their children. I disagree with them, of course, but I believe truly concerned parents and guardians deserve compassion, even if they express anger toward you that causes you a lot of wobble. Again, I'm talking about extending compassion toward parents and guardians who are concerned about their child, not those who want to threaten you because of ideological differences.

Even if you don't want to extend compassion toward those parents and guardians who make your life stressful, you may find practicing compassion and responding to these parents and guardians with compassion to be useful. As the late Marshall Rosenberg (2015) argued, just as our emotions can give us insight into our values and unmet needs, the emotions that other people express to us give us insight into their values and needs. According to Rosenberg's framework for communication, called nonviolent communication, when both sides of a conflict understand the other's unmet needs and requests, the chances of successfully resolving conflicts are improved. If you can determine what an angry parent really wants and respond to their needs with compassionate understanding, you will have more success in dealing with them. I don't mean that you must give in to their requests, but if you can have a dialogue with them in which you communicate compassionately and demonstrate an understanding for their perspective, I believe things will go more smoothly for you than if you did not respond with compassion.

Just as wobble presents opportunities for growth, conflict between you and a parent or guardian presents you with an exciting opportunity. Rosenberg (2015) views conflict, like the kind created from receiving an email from an angry parent, as "an opportunity to enrich someone's life" (p. 100). You might not be very interested in enriching the life of an angry parent or guardian, especially the first time (or 100 times) you read their email, but extending compassion toward them gives you the opportunity to make a positive difference in their life. CLP encourages people to act to make the world better; your compassionate responses to angry parents and guardians can help make the world a better place. If you've decided to try extending compassion to your students' parents or guardians, remember, you must first practice compassion for self.

Practice Practicing

Teaching, like yoga, is a never-ending practice. No matter how many years of experience an educator has, they can still improve. This is not a negative thing. It means that educators are lucky enough to have a career with constant opportunities for growth and improvement, which can add meaning and fulfillment to our lives.

The concept of stretchiness for wobble that I discussed in this book is also not a negative thing. A teacher's current readiness and commitment to teaching for CHANGE is exactly that—their current readiness and commitment. If, while reading this book, you've felt that your stretchiness for wobble right now will not allow you to enact CLP in the ways I've described, please keep practicing mindfulness and compassion for self. If you do not feel prepared for the wobbles you anticipate right now, that is okay! Keep teaching, and with each new year or new unit, please practice expanding your stretchiness. With time, reflection, compassion, and support from your colleagues and loved ones, you can expand your stretchiness for wobble. You can grow personally and professionally because of the wobbles you experience. Any attempts you make to teach for CHANGE will help you improve your practice. Keep it up!

Concluding Encouragement

I hope reading this book has inspired you in your efforts to promote critical literacy with your students. Further, I hope that you've been encouraged to accept moments of wobble caused from teaching for CHANGE as exciting opportunities. Wobbling doesn't have to make you suffer. Remember, experiencing wobble presents you with opportunities to grow and flow. Enacting CLP is a worthwhile goal to pursue, and the challenges you face can help you enjoy the pursuit. Working with your students to change the world to make it more just and equitable can bring joy and fulfillment to you and your students. Go CHANGE the world with them.

References

Csikszentmihalyi, M. (1990). *Flow: The psychology of optimal experience*. Harper & Row.

Fecho, B., Graham, P., & Hudson-Ross, S. (2005). Appreciating the wobble: Teacher research, professional development, and figured worlds. *English Education, 37*(3), 174–199.

Garcia, A., & O'Donnell-Allen, C. (2015). *Pose, wobble, flow: A culturally proactive approach to literacy instruction*. Teachers College Press.

Hanh, T. N. (2015). *The heart of the Buddha's teaching: Transforming suffering into peace, joy, and liberation*. Harmony.

Richo, D. (1991). *How to be an adult: A handbook on psychological and spiritual integration*. Paulist Press.

Rosenberg, M. B. (2015). *Nonviolent communication: A language of life* (3rd ed.). PuddleDancer Press.

Appendix A: Suggestions for Teaching for CHANGE in English Language Arts

Regardless of which grade(s) you teach, the following suggestions can help you assess your teaching and curriculum to discover opportunities to teach for CHANGE. I suggest you engage in critical self-reflection, evaluate your curriculum, and explore professional organizations that can support you. Teaching for CHANGE requires educators to challenge the status quo, and sadly, racism continues to influence the ways that English language arts (ELA) is taught in U.S. schools (see Baker-Bell, 2020; Johnson, 2022; Wellington & Walker, 2023). Therefore, I believe teaching for CHANGE begins with critical self-reflection so teachers can evaluate their own biases and (re)dedicate themselves to anti-racist teaching.

Engage in Critical Self-Reflection

I suggest you perform what Sealey-Ruiz (2022) calls "Archaeology of the Self," which she describes as a "deep excavation and exploration of beliefs, biases, and ideas" that impact your teaching (p. 22). In her article, Sealey-Ruiz provides resources teachers can use to support their archaeology of the self. I suggest you read her article and also consider reading some of the resources she provides. Wellington and Walker (2023) provide suggestions and resources to help teachers remain committed to anti-racist teaching practices. Building on the work of other scholars and researchers, they view anti-racist teaching as pedagogy that is dedicated to resisting White supremacy; to dismantling racism, not just acknowledging that it exists but doing something "to take action against it" (p. 27); and to supporting students of color in their own empowerment. The following questions may support you in critical self-reflection:

- How do I view my students and their literacies (i.e., the ways they use language and text to accomplish their goals)?
- Do I have low expectations of my students who are not labeled as "gifted"?
- Do I have low expectations of my students of color?
- Whose voices and perspectives do I privilege in my classroom, and whose voices and perspectives do I ignore or silence?
- Do I consistently provide anti-racist teaching, or is this an area I must improve in?
- What needed changes to my perspectives and teaching does this critical self-reflection reveal, and how can I begin to make those changes?
- What do I need to learn or research to make these needed changes?

Evaluate Your Curriculum

Before a new school year or before you start a new unit, consider evaluating what you are planning to teach next. Evaluating your curriculum can reveal exciting opportunities to teach for CHANGE. Please ask your peers who teach the same courses as you to participate in this curriculum assessment with you. Collaboration is a wonderful way to discover even more opportunities to teach for CHANGE. Here are some questions I suggest you consider:

- What injustices occurring in your state or county might connect with texts you will be teaching? How can you support students in using the texts you're planning to teach "as tools of critique and resistance" (Morrell, 2008, p. 31)?

- What additional texts could you easily connect to the ones you're already teaching that could engage students in critical literacy?
- How can you diversify the texts you read in your curriculum to reflect your students' lives, literacies, and cultures?
- What writing assignments do you have students do? Are they for real audiences? Could these assignments be revised slightly to get students writing for CHANGE?
- Is there a class project students could do that still addresses the required standards and helps students learn the content, literacies, and skills valued in your curriculum but also engages them in making a CHANGE in the world surrounding them?

I recognize that you and your peers may have set curricula you are required to teach. When I taught secondary ELA, the district provided curriculum maps I was expected to follow, and this limited my options. You too might teach in a restrictive context that offers you less autonomy. If that is the case, please still consider finding small changes you can make to your curriculum that will allow you to provide critical literacy pedagogy.

Explore Professional Organizations that Can Support Your Efforts

I need to disclose that I am a member of the National Council of Teachers of English (NCTE), and I will serve on the NCTE Secondary Section Steering Committee starting in November 2024. The NCTE offers free online resources for teachers, like their position statements. One position statement that secondary ELA teachers hoping to teach for CHANGE may find useful as book-banning efforts are on the rise (see Limbong, 2022) is the "The Students' Right to Read" (NCTE, 2018). Another online resource available to members is the "This Story Matters" database (NCTE, n.d.). NCTE members can use this database to access over 1,000 rationales written for classroom teachers and school librarians to defend their book selections. The NCTE also publishes academic journals, like the *English Journal*, which members can access. The Sealey-Ruiz (2022) and Wellington and Walker (2023) articles cited above were both published in the *English Journal*. The NCTE has been invaluable to me as an educator, and I highly recommend that secondary ELA teachers join the NCTE as well.

References

Baker-Bell, A. (2020). *Linguist justice: Black Language, literacy, identity, and pedagogy*. Routledge.

Johnson, L. J. (2022). *Critical race English education: New visions, new possibilities*. Routledge.

Limbong, A. (2022, September 19). *New report finds a coordinated rise in attempted book bans*. NPR. https://www.npr.org/2022/09/19/1123156201/new-report-finds-a-coordinated-rise-in-attempted-bok-bans

Morrell, E. (2008). *Critical literacy and urban youth: Pedagogies of access, dissent, and liberation*. Routledge.

National Council of Teachers of English. (2018, October 25). *The students' right to read.* https://ncte.org/statement/righttoreadguideline/

National Council of Teachers of English. (n.d.). *This story matters: Standing up for students' right to read in the face of censorship*. Retrieved February 27, 2024, from https://ncte.org/book-rationales/this-story-matters/

Sealey-Ruiz, Y. S. (2022). An archaeology of self for our times: Another talk to teachers. *English Journal, 111*(5), 21–26. https://doi.org/10.58680/ej202231819

Wellington, D., & Walker, A. (2023). Reimagining teaching for hope and justice: Teaching practices for an anti-racist classroom. *English Journal, **113***(1), 25–31. https://doi.org/10.58680/ej202332627

Appendix B: Example Letter to Parents and Guardians about Your Plans for the R&J Issues Unit

Dear Parents and Guardians,

    I'm very excited to study Shakespeare's *Romeo and Juliet* with your child in their English class in the coming weeks. While this classic play is often taught in high school, I'll be teaching it slightly differently, so I wanted to reach out to you first to explain what we will be doing in class and why we will be doing it. I anticipate you may have some concerns or questions. Please read this whole letter, and if you still have concerns about what your child will be studying in my class, please call me at # or email me at @. You can also contact my administrator at @.

    Recently, I have been concerned about book-banning efforts across multiple states in the country which have resulted in books being banned from classrooms and school libraries. I have been concerned, not because your child's safety and health are unimportant to me but because book-banning efforts often ignore the voices and opinions of the people who will be most impacted by a book ban: your child. Students are rarely trusted to make important decisions about what is or is not appropriate for them to read, and they are often not consulted when books are being banned. I am also concerned about book bans because many "classic" texts often studied in school contain sexual innuendoes, violence, teen suicide, and other questionable content. Yet these texts are not currently the ones most likely to be challenged. The ones most likely to be challenged are those written for youth, like young adult novels, that your child probably would rather read than a "classic."

I've also been concerned recently about the relevance of studying *Romeo and Juliet* in this age of artificial intelligence and YouTube videos that can summarize the entire play in less time than it takes to read five pages of it. I'm concerned that if I don't do something that students find meaningful, they will struggle to stay motivated to read and study the play and that if I don't make my class more interesting, your child won't learn anything in it. I want your child to learn as much as they can in my class.

Considering these concerns, I've worked with the other grade 9 English teachers to create a unit on *Romeo and Juliet* that we think is relevant, engaging, appropriate, and meaningful to your child. We want to use our unit on Shakespeare's *Romeo and Juliet* to help your child to understand the play, to help your child participate actively in their learning, and to help them think critically for themselves. We will still cover the required standards and teach your child the skills they need to be successful in their English language arts (ELA) class, in their future ELA classes, and beyond.

During this unit, your child will choose a young adult novel from a list of recently challenged books. These books have been challenged because they feature sex scenes, teen romance, and teen suicide. I want to point out a few things: First, *Romeo and Juliet* also features violence, teenage sex, and suicide. You might remember from your high school days that Romeo is an older teenager and Juliet is only 13. They have sex before they die by suicide, all behind their parents' backs. So your child will already be exposed to some heavy content as we study the play, which has been taught at this school for decades. Second, your child will choose a book to read that has been challenged, not an officially banned book. It would be inappropriate for me to make available to your child a book that has been banned by the state or district. A challenged book, however, is simply a book that people have questioned whether it is appropriate for teens to read. I am attaching to this letter a list of the books your child can choose from, so you can know what they will be reading on their own.

Your child will read the book they choose on their own, and they will evaluate their selected book to determine if they think it was appropriate or not. In class, we will have several discussions to determine if we think *Romeo and Juliet* was an appropriate text for us to study. Your child's main assignment for this unit on *Romeo and Juliet* will be to write an argumentative essay evaluating the appropriateness for school of both the play and the novel they read. Your child will engage in critical thinking as they read an entire novel on their own. I know that you may be concerned about the book they choose to read, but please remember they can always choose a different book to complete if you or they decide the first one they selected is inappropriate. Remember also the purpose of reading a challenged book is not to be rebellious or to harm your child. They are reading it to evaluate it and contribute to this very important discussion about which texts are appropriate for students to read in school and which ones are not. I believe your child should have a say in this debate. Also, think about how wonderful it will be for your child to read an entire novel on their own! This unit gives them a purpose to read that will likely help motivate them to accomplish that difficult task.

If you are concerned about a young adult novel that features teen sex or suicide, I completely understand. This might be tough to consider, but research indicates many teens are sexually active in high school, and some have experienced nonconsensual sexual activity. While this might be an uncomfortable topic for you to think about or discuss with your child, it is important for your child who is in their first year in high school to be aware of teen sexual activity and the issue of consent. I know I am not your child's sex ed teacher, but when we are studying a text that features teenage sex, I am obligated to address the important issue of sexual consent because I care about your child. I don't want something we study in class to convey harmful messages to your child. The same applies to teen suicide. Since Romeo and Juliet die by suicide in the play, I must discuss teen suicide delicately with your child as we study the play. In class, we will address teen suicide in a healthy way that appreciates the severity of the topic. I am also collaborating with school counselors to make supportive resources available to students, and you should know I am a mandatory reporter. If your child mentions having suicidal thoughts, I am obligated by law to report this.

Finally, some of the books on the list that your child can choose from feature characters who are members of LGBTQIA+ communities. First, I want to say clearly that I am an ally for LGBTQIA+ students and I want all students to feel safe, welcomed, and valued in my class. This does not mean, however, that I believe it is my job to make your child think a certain way or read a book they don't want to read. You are their parent or guardian, and I respect your rights. I also respect your child. The only major text I am "forcing" your child to read is *Romeo and Juliet*. They will choose the novel they read, and, of course, you should help them make their choice. As you help them make this choice, though, please consider the following: According to a research brief developed by The Trevor Project, LGBTQIA+ youth who interact with accepting adults are less likely to attempt suicide than their peers who did not have support from adults. Reading a book like Mike Curato's *Flamer* could help LGBTQIA+ youth (whether they are out or not), who are more likely to experience suicidal thoughts than their peers. I know you care about your child, so please consider the potential benefit to them of helping them in choosing to read a book that supports LGBTQIA+ youth.

Thank you for reading this letter. I know it was a lot, but I wanted to share my passion for your child's learning and the reasoning behind this unit. I hope you see that your child's learning and well-being are important to me. If I just taught this play the way it has been taught in the past, your child would learn little that isn't on the internet. Helping your child engage in critical and evaluative thinking that compares and contrasts multiple texts and results in their writing a coherent argument that cites evidence to support their main points, though—well, I hope you see how that's going to be much more meaningful to them and much more important for their education than answering questions like "Who said, 'O Romeo, Romeo, wherefore art thou Romeo?'"

Appendix C: Example Letter to Parents or Guardians about Your Plans for the Speaking into the Silence Unit

Dear Parents and Guardians,

    This year we will be studying a new novel in your child's English class. We'll be reading *American Street* by Ibi Zoboi. This is a young adult novel that explores themes related to family relationships, coming of age, and dealing with change and hardship. I am excited to teach this novel because I think students will really enjoy it. It is a compelling story that will hopefully motivate your child to read it. The novel addresses issues regarding immigration because the protagonist Fabiola is a U.S. citizen, but her mother is Haitian. Fabiola's mother is detained by U.S. immigration at the beginning of the novel when the pair of them try to come back to the United States from Haiti. The novel includes profanity, characters who sell drugs, an abusive relationship, and death. You can read about the book on the author's website (https://www.ibizoboi.net/american-street). I anticipate you may have some concerns about the content of this new novel and what lessons I'll be teaching. Please read this whole letter, and if you still have concerns about what your child will be studying in my class, please call me at # or email me at @. You can also contact my administrator at @.

    The other grade 10 English language arts (ELA) teachers and I have created a unit to teach this novel for several reasons. First, we believe students should encounter diverse characters and experiences in their schooling. We also believe that texts studied in school should operate as mirrors and windows for students.

As respected professor Rudine Sims Bishop argued, students deserve to see themselves reflected in the texts they study in school (mirrors), and students also deserve opportunities to read about characters who are different from them (windows). In *American Street*, which is written by a Haitian American, Fabiola lives with her aunt and cousins in Detroit as she waits to be reunited with her mother. Many students at our school may find Fabiola to be a kind of mirror for them, even if they are not from Haiti. For our students who did not immigrate to the U.S., this novel can serve as a window for them to learn about immigrant experiences while still reading a novel that they can relate to.

The other grade 10 ELA teachers and I also created this unit because we wanted to help our students explore events, issues, cultures, and experiences that they may not know much about just yet. Because Fabiola immigrates from Haiti, we know we will need to teach our students a little about Haitian history and culture. As we prepared to do that, we realized that Haitian history and culture are very important to U.S. history and culture, but a lot of people do not know that. We realized that the study of Haitian history has been ignored in schooling, and we wondered what else mattered to our students that has also been ignored. The main assignment of this unit, therefore, is a research project. Your child will select an event, issue, or culture that they feel has been ignored from their schooling that they would like to know more about. They will research it and present their research to the class. I am excited for what your child will learn as they complete their project!

I realize, though, that my perspective and approach may come across as overly negative. As we study the novel, we will discuss past racism that occurred during the colonization of Haiti as well as past racism that occurred in Detroit since the novel takes place there. We will also discuss current examples of racism. I don't want us to discuss racism to make any students uncomfortable or to promote an anti-American attitude. However, I believe strongly that students should have opportunities in school to discuss important issues and consider different perspectives so they can be more informed and involved citizens. Recently, there have been efforts to silence classrooms discussions of race and racism in schools. Still, educators across the nation, including the National Association of Teachers of English, which is a nationwide professional organization, believe it is our duty to engage students in these difficult but crucial conversations. The National Association of Teachers of English produced a position statement on antiracist teaching, which states, "Teaching racial histories and antiracist education do not constitute anti-Americanism but serve as one element in an education that supports the development of informed citizens who can work toward a more equitable society." Because I agree with their position statement, I have included the entire statement with this letter so you can read more about my perspective on discussing racism in school. I especially agree with their point that ELA teachers have a responsibility to promote antiracist education. An antiracist education does *not* mean I will make White students in my classroom feel guilty for the racist thoughts and actions of others. An antiracist education <u>does</u> mean that, when it is relevant to the texts we're studying in class, we address racist actions and thoughts, be they past or present, and call them what they are: racist.

I want to point out that we used to read Harper Lee's *To Kill a Mockingbird* in grade 10 ELA. Your child would have discussed racism if we were still reading that novel. As I teach this new unit, I plan to remind students that texts are written by people who have their own beliefs and biases. Your child will not be forced to believe anything they do not want to believe, nor will they be discriminated against. I have rules that I enforce in class to ensure that students demonstrate respect for each other. Your child may, however, read some texts that offer a perspective different from their own. That is one of the benefits of an education: It exposes a person to different ideas and ways of viewing the world, but in my classroom, I respect your child and their rights to their own views. I also respect you and your rights; that's why I'm writing you this letter.

Finally, you may be concerned about this new unit on *American Street* because it contains profanity or because of some of the decisions that characters make. (Fabiola's cousins decide to sell drugs to try to help their mother financially.) I surveyed the class before I wrote this letter, and it seems that most students in my class hear or use profanity roughly [insert data from survey] at school daily. When we read the novel in class, I may ask students not to read certain words aloud. As my informal survey data shows, though, profanity is not really anything new for your child. The survey also revealed that students in your child's ELA class have seen movies or shows about dealing drugs, so I do not think this mature content is anything they cannot handle. Please reach out to me with any concerns you have.

Thank you for taking the time to read this letter. I hope it conveys to you how much your child's education means to me and how excited I am for what your child will learn from studying this new book and from conducting their research. Fabiola learns important life lessons about family, making tough decisions, and navigating change in *American Street*, and I believe your child will learn some of those lessons too! I'm passionate about making my ELA class meaningful to students because I believe that's one of the best ways to help them learn, not only ELA but also more about themselves.

Appendix D: Example Letter to Parents or Guardians about Your Plans for the Environmental Justice Unit

Dear Parents and Guardians,

This year, we will be studying a new novel in your child's English class: Helena María Viramontes's *Under the Feet of Jesus*. This novel, like John Steinbeck's *Of Mice and Men*, explores the injustices and abuses experienced by migrant farmworkers in California. Unlike *Of Mice and Men*, Viramontes's novel takes place in the 1990s and features Mexican-American characters. As we study the novel, we will consider themes often explored in American Literature courses (like how to respond to injustice, the consequences of abusing power, and concerns about humanity's impact on nature). We will also address concerns specific to the novel, like the ways immigrant farmworkers have been and continue to be abused by agribusiness in the United States. As we read, I'm planning to use the following question to guide our discussions and responses to the novel: How are some of the injustices in the novel still happening today, and what can we do about it?

I anticipate that you may have some concerns about the content of this new novel and what lessons I'll be teaching. Please read this whole letter, and if you still have concerns about what your child will be studying in my class, please call me at # or email me at @. You can also contact my administrator at @.

Your child's English course this year focuses on American literature. The curriculum highlights the ways that Americans have advocated for needed change. Already this year, your child has read excerpts of *The Declaration of Independence* to analyze how

Thomas Jefferson and other founders used rhetoric to argue convincingly for needed change. Your child has also read about Dr. Martin Luther King, Jr.'s nonviolent approaches to advocate for change in the past. I plan to use this unit to help your child think of ways they can be involved in advocating for change today.

I understand you may be concerned that I am pushing a political agenda on your child. I want you to know that I respect you and your child. It is not my job to tell your child what to think. It is my job, though, to engage your child in meaningful learning that they can use in class and beyond the walls of the classroom. I believe that no class curriculum is neutral or devoid of political implications. The texts I typically teach in my American Literature courses were written by people with diverse political views, religious beliefs, and ideologies. The authors we study wrote during times of revolution, change, upheaval, peace, and war. Any text that could fall under the umbrella of "American Literature" will therefore represent diverse values and ideologies, all with political implications. This does not mean, however, that I will impose my views on your child. That would be inappropriate and against my philosophy of education.

What I'm most excited about in this new unit is that your child will work with their classmates to plan ways they can be engaged in activism that matters to them and that they decide on together. I will support them and guide them in this process, but I want them to make the important decisions, as I believe doing so will engage them in meaningful work that will excite them and motivate them in their learning.

Recently, I was dismayed when I read a report by the Pew Research Center stating that 58% of high school teachers said that "students showing little or no interest in learning is a major problem in their classroom." I don't blame students when I read this. Instead, I ask myself, "What changes can I make to my teaching to make my class more interesting so my students are engaged in their learning?" I don't want your child to be bored or uninterested in my class! I believe that this new unit will excite your child by encouraging them to get involved in activism, which makes studying the novel more relevant to them than the ways I have taught novels in the past.

Thank you for taking the time to read this letter. I hope it conveys to you how excited I am to provide engaging lessons that get your child thinking critically and advocating for change. The study of American Literature is the study of inspirational people who noticed something that needed to be changed and used their words (and actions) to make that change happen. I'm looking forward to being inspired by your child and their classmates as we study *Under the Feet of Jesus* this year.

Appendix E: Example Letter to Parents or Guardians about Your Plans for the Postcolonial Literature Unit

Dear Parents and Guardians,

I'm thrilled to be your child's English teacher for their senior year! This is such an exciting (and stressful) time for them (and for you). I'm writing this letter to let you know that this year we will be studying a new novel. Because the grade 12 curriculum emphasizes British literature, which many of my former students have told me was boring, I wanted to teach a novel that I think will interest them. This year, in addition to plenty of the "classic" British literature texts, I'll be teaching Tsitsi Dangarembga's novel *The Book of Not*. Dangarembga is a Zimbabwean author. Zimbabwe was previously colonized by the British, and Dangarembga's novel focuses on the main character's journey through secondary school as well as the challenges she faces after graduating and trying to establish a career for herself. I believe this novel, though it takes place in the 1970s on a different continent, has themes that are extremely relevant for your child.

The Book of Not is considered a postcolonial text because it was written by a person from a formerly colonized country and because Dangarembga's book details the ways that British colonial attitudes impacted the Black characters. Because it is a postcolonial work, the novel addresses racism and colonialist attitudes that many Europeans living in Zimbabwe held when it was a British colony. When we study this novel, we will discuss heavy topics, but your child is a senior now, and I'm confident they are mature enough to handle anything that comes up in class.

One of the reasons I wanted to teach this new novel is that the main character becomes disillusioned after she graduates from high school and is unable to achieve her goals that she thought would bring her happiness and fulfillment. Your child will graduate soon, and I don't want them to experience that same disillusionment and disappointment. So, as we study the novel, your child will do some research on their own. The main project during this unit requires your child to research what they think will bring them happiness and fulfillment in life. They will read articles, maybe even some books, and interview their classmates, family members (I hope they'll interview you), and other influential people in their lives to explore what can bring them fulfillment as they mature into adulthood. I can't wait to hear what your child and their classmates learn as they engage in this important inquiry. I hope studying this novel will excite your child as they are about to begin the next chapter of their lives.

If you have concerns or questions about the content of this new novel and what lessons I'll be teaching, please feel free to call me at # or email me at @. You can also contact my administrator at @.

For Product Safety Concerns and Information please contact our EU representative GPSR@taylorandfrancis.com
Taylor & Francis Verlag GmbH, Kaufingerstraße 24, 80331 München, Germany

www.ingramcontent.com/pod-product-compliance
Lightning Source LLC
Chambersburg PA
CBHW062224300426
44115CB00012BA/2214